BENJAMIN FRANKLIN EXPLAINS THE STAMP ACT PROTESTS TO PARLIAMENT, 1766

Peter Charles Hoffer

DIALOGUES IN HISTORY

Series Editors
Peter Charles Hoffer
Williamjames Hull Hoffer

Benjamin Franklin Explains the Stamp Act Protests to Parliament, 1766

PETER CHARLES HOFFER

NEW YORK | OXFORD
Oxford University Press

Oxford University Press is a department of the University of Oxford.
It furthers the University's objective of excellence in research,
scholarship, and education by publishing worldwide.

Oxford New York
Auckland Cape Town Dar es Salaam Hong Kong Karachi
Kuala Lumpur Madrid Melbourne Mexico City Nairobi
New Delhi Shanghai Taipei Toronto

With offices in
Argentina Austria Brazil Chile Czech Republic France Greece
Guatemala Hungary Italy Japan Poland Portugal Singapore
South Korea Switzerland Thailand Turkey Ukraine Vietnam

For titles covered by Section 112 of the US Higher Education Opportunity Act, please visit www.oup.com/us/he for the latest information about pricing and alternate formats.

Published by Oxford University Press
198 Madison Avenue, New York, New York 10016
http://www.oup.com

Library of Congress Cataloging-in-Publication Data
Hoffer, Peter Charles, 1944-
Benjamin Franklin explains the Stamp Act protests to Parliament, 1766 / Peter Charles Hoffer.
pages cm. -- (Dialogues in history)
Includes bibliographical references and index.
ISBN 978-0-19-938968-1 (paperback)
1. Great Britain. Stamp Act (1765) 2. Franklin, Benjamin, 1706–1790--Political and social views. 3. United States--Relations--Great Britain--Sources. 4. Great Britain--Relations--United States--Sources. 5. Great Britain--Colonies--America--History--18th century--Sources. 6. Great Britain. Parliament--History--18th century--Sources. 7. Protest movements--United States--History--18th century--Sources. 8. United States--Politics and government--To 1775--Sources. I. Title.
E215.2.H63 2016
973.3'111--dc23

2014029519

Printing number: 9 8 7 6 5 4 3 2 1

Printed in the United States of America
on acid-free paper

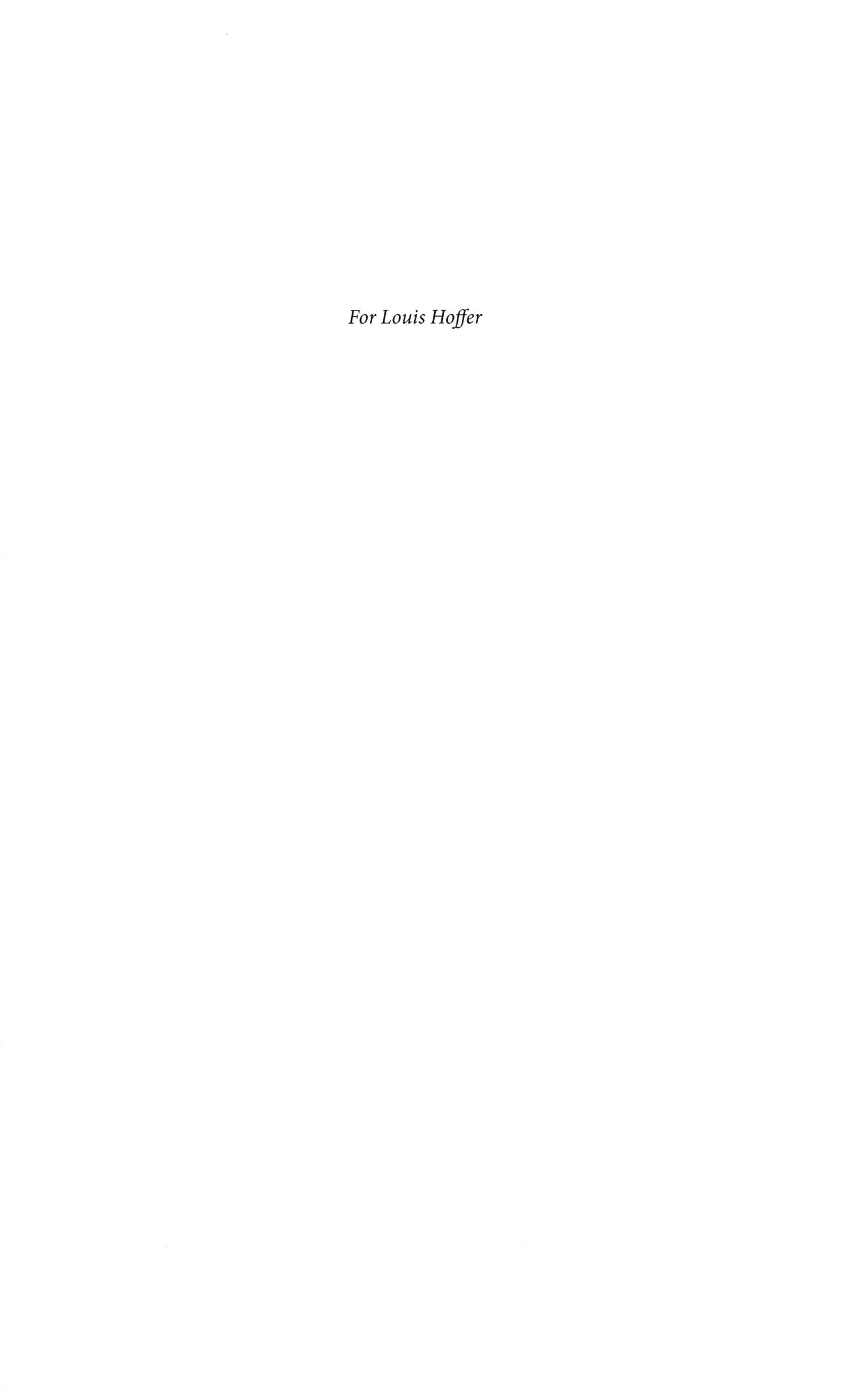

For Louis Hoffer

Contents

Preface

THIS COLLECTION OF documents on the Stamp Act, at the center of which is Benjamin Franklin's examination in Parliament on February 13, 1766, is meant to be read as a continuous dialogue among leading colonists in America and politicians in England. While the individual documents were separated in time and space, they here are reconstituted as part of a consistent whole—a trans-Atlantic conversation about the nature of the empire, the rights of the colonists, and the powers of Parliament at a critical moment in American and British history. Some liberty has been taken in their editing to emphasize this conversational quality. Their chronological order and their context in the larger debate has not been altered. The ideal is to make history come alive. Novelists do this by inventing dialogue. Historians do not have this license, but in this series of books they can rearrange dialogue to enhance its pedagogical effectiveness.

No set of primary sources can fully convey the richness and variety of the argument over the stamp tax, but that is not the purpose of this collection. Instead, here the drama and commitment of the speakers is moved to center stage, giving a reader a sense of what was at stake in the minds of the participants. A chronology preceding the documents indicates the sequence of their production, and a bibliographical essay at the end of the documents directs the reader to useful secondary sources.

To help the dialogue come to life, the authors allow themselves certain liberties with the unwrapping of the sources. For example, in the present volume, I wrote that late in the examination Franklin "must have been deeply tired." How could I know this? Well, he had been standing for nearly three hours, answering questions that literally came at him from all sides of the Commons chamber. He was a heavy-set sixty-year-old, and the whole process must have been an ordeal. Surely he was deeply tired; who would not have been? Similar commonsense inferences and commentary are interspersed within the documents as a kind of running commentary or voice-over.

The author gratefully acknowledges the assistance of Steven Berry, Benjamin Ehlers, Williamjames Hull Hoffer, and Michael Winship in preparing the format for this volume, the readers of the proposal for the series at Oxford University Press, and the readers of the present volume, Peter Messer, John Reda, and John G. McCurdy, for their valuable suggestions.

At the press, Brian Wheel once again understood immediately the novelty and the applicability of the series. Cindy Sweeny and Wendy Walker oversaw the copy-editing, and Taylor Pilkington and Gina Bocchetta facilitated production of the work.

BENJAMIN FRANKLIN EXPLAINS THE STAMP ACT PROTESTS TO PARLIAMENT, 1766

Peter Charles Hoffer

INTRODUCTION

The Colonists Protest the Stamp Act

HISTORIANS OF THE American Revolution agree that the protests over the Stamp Act from the winter and spring of 1765 through the repeal of the Act on March 23, 1766, were a major turning point in American popular politics, American political thought, and the resistance movement against British colonial governance. They were also a turning point in British history, the beginning of the end of the old British empire. Benjamin Franklin played a controversial part in both of those stories. Resident in London, he had privately warned against the legislation, then accepted it and promoted a friend in Philadelphia for one of the lucrative distributorships, then turned about again and orchestrated a campaign for repeal of the Act in which he played a more visible role.

On Thursday, February 13, 1766, the portly, sixty-year-old Franklin stood in the well of the House of Commons, in Westminster, England, and explained American resistance to the Act to the members of Parliament. Some of the members were angry, others bewildered at the widespread violent protests against the Act they had passed but a year previously, but most were resigned to the eventuality of repeal. A few were Franklin's friends and confidants. All were curious: Why had Americans so vehemently opposed what had seemed to their imperial rulers such a straightforward way to recover from the fiscal crisis of the day? The dialogue between Franklin and the members reached back to the triumph of British and American arms in the last great war for empire and forward to the day when Americans would chafe at the bit of empire.[1]

The French and Indian War (called the Seven Years' War in Europe) of 1754–1763 enmeshed the British in combat on every continent except Australia and Antarctica. It was the last in a series of wars pitting Britain and its allies against France and its allies in Europe and the American colonies, but instead of beginning in Europe and traveling to the colonies, it began in the west of the colony of Pennsylvania and two years later erupted in Europe. Victory and peace brought Britain all of French Canada and New France, a territory stretching from the Acadian Peninsula across to the Great Lakes and down the Mississippi River to the border of Louisiana. It also emptied the British treasury. William Pitt, the leader of King George II's government in Parliament and the Secretary of State for the Southern Department (the minister of state with direct authority over the colonies), had done what needed to be done to defend the colonies against Britain's imperial rivals, but his arbitrary and abrupt manner did not appeal to the young King George III. George III replaced Pitt with Lord Bute, an advisor to the Crown. News of the peace brought celebration throughout the British colonies, but Britain still faced a myriad of problems. To sort these out, George III replaced Bute with a career administrator and lawyer, George Grenville. This pompous, long-winded, and incorruptible civil servant was not popular in government circles, but his competence with money matters made him valuable at a time when English public finances were in dire straits.[2]

George Grenville (1712–1770), mezzotint from a portrait by William Hoare, circa 1765.

Grenville committed himself and his parliamentary supporters to a program of cutting expenses and increasing revenues. To that end, they downsized the royal army and navy (save for troops stationed in the Great Lakes area), but the problem of increasing the income of the Crown remained. It appeared to Grenville that colonial merchants violated the Navigation Acts with impunity and ignored the instructions of the Board of Trade. The Navigation Acts were a series of parliamentary enactments going back to the 1650s that regulated trade within the empire, required that colonial shippers use British or colonial vessels, prohibited commerce with countries not part of the British empire, and "enumerated" certain staple goods like tobacco that had to be shipped directly to British ports. Despite revenue gained from the Navigation Acts, the English national debt had doubled in the course of the 1750s, in large measure to support the war effort in the North American colonies. Colonial smuggling (a violation of the Navigation Acts that colonial merchants and shippers routinely practiced) cost the customs service as much as £700,000 a year. It was time to "reform" the empire by forcing the colonies to obey their imperial rulers and pay their fair share of the cost of the empire.[3]

With financial disaster looming in the winter of 1763–1764, Grenville and his supporters decided on a legislative means to raise a revenue from the colonies. A revision of the Molasses Act of 1733, scheduled to expire in 1764, seemed an obvious place to raise a revenue and remind the colonists of their duties. The Sugar Act (American Revenue Act) of 1764 placed a tariff on legal importation of molasses, rum, and raw sugar from non-British colonies. Grenville proposed to lower the duty on foreign molasses to three pence per gallon but to enforce its collection; to increase the duties on coffee, indigo, and wines imported directly into the colonies; and to add iron, hides, silk, potash, pearl ash, and whale fins to the list of enumerated articles (colonial goods that were to be shipped directly to British ports). The sweetener in the deal was the provision that all monies raised from the duties were "reserved, to be, from time to time, disposed of by parliament, towards defraying the necessary expences of defending, protecting, and securing, the British colonies and plantations in America." The problem was the legislation had forty-seven clauses, some so complicated that colonial merchants would have no idea what traps it had set for them. Grenville introduced the measure in Parliament on March 9, 1764, and it passed on April 5, 1764.[4]

To colonial waters Grenville ordered eight warships and twelve armed sloops to enforce the Act, adding the possibility of fiscal injury to the existing insult to the honor of colonial merchants. The New England merchants protested, to no avail. But the new Act did not fill the English treasury. Grenville may or may not have invited important colonists sojourning in England to suggest other means of raising a revenue than a direct tax, including some form of subsidy the colonies would provide for their own defense by British forces. Grenville may or may not have given some encouragement to these agents—at least some of them believed that he had done so. Or the entire episode may have been one of the many misunderstandings that preceded Grenville's determination to impose a stamp tax on the colonies, for the agents of the various colonial legislatures sent to London must have known that "their constituents would grumble at the proposed parliamentary stamp tax. Two of the colonies, New York and Massachusetts, had tried stamp taxes levied by their own assemblies and had later discarded them as unsatisfactory. Furthermore, there would probably be objections to any tax imposed on the colonies by Parliament. The colonists would be able to argue, with some plausibility, that all taxes hitherto had been levied by the colonial assemblies with the exception of duties for regulation of trade," but Grenville was not disposed to hear any challenge to Parliament's right to tax the colonies.[5]

In early 1765, Grenville told Parliament that he "hoped that the power and sovereignty of Parliament, over every part of the British dominions, for the purpose of raising or collecting any tax, would never be disputed," and on February 6, 1765, Grenville brought the bill to the House of Commons. According to the Act, the tax would fall on "every skin, or piece of vellum or parchment, or sheet or piece of paper," including legal documents, newspapers, and even tavern keepers' licenses, angering the men and women who dominated local politics in many towns and cities.[6]

The bill, passed in Parliament on February 27, 1765, and signed by the king a month later, was designed to raise revenue in America. Americans were required to use pre-embossed paper, supplied by ship from England. The colonial agents had warned that such a direct tax on the colonists would be resisted. In February 1765, Franklin himself, representing Pennsylvania, had tried to convince Grenville not to present the bill to Parliament—ironic in light of Franklin's inclusion of a very similar scheme of taxation in his Albany Plan of Union of 1754. But neither Grenville, whose idea the Act was, nor anyone in Parliament (including the handful of members of the House of Commons who voted against the bill), nor the colonists who agreed to serve as distributors of the stamped paper anticipated the virulence of the colonial response.[7]

While it was true that Grenville and his supporters were not really concerned with popular opinion, whether in England or the colonies, in fact many in England would support his program. Only a few would object that the colonies should be allowed to tax themselves. In the colonies, however, there was general opposition to Grenville's ideas.

What happened to Massachusetts Lieutenant Governor Thomas Hutchinson was an example of how a well-established merchant and royal official with ties to the first families of the colony fared in the face the anti-stamp movement. He saw his duty as an officer of the Crown and he saw his opportunities for advancement. Given his place in the government in 1765, as Chief Justice of the Massachusetts Superior Court of Judicature and Lieutenant Governor of the colony, it was his duty to support the new imposts that Grenville and his ministry in England had shepherded through Parliament. Hutchinson personally opposed the tax, but he knew a good patronage opportunity when he saw it, and urged merchant Andrew

Stamp Act protests in Boston.

Oliver, his brother-in-law, to take advantage of the fees that would come to the stamp distributor in the colony.[8]

While Massachusetts' General Court drafted petitions against the Act, the "loyal nine," a group of Boston merchants led by Samuel Adams and none of them friends to Hutchinson, roused the South Boston gang, led by Ebenezer McIntosh, a cobbler by trade and a bone crusher by avocation, to pressure the new stamp collector to resign his commission. Together these men, later calling themselves "Sons of Liberty," engaged in public demonstrations against the hated Act even before its details were known in the colony.[9]

On the night of August 13, the ringleaders stuffed a cloth effigy of Oliver with rags and hanged it on a "liberty tree" (the celebrated name came later), a giant elm under whose high leafy arms thousands could gather, at the corner of modern Washington and Essex streets. The effigy had notes pinned to it, denouncing those who subverted liberty and various doggerel rhymes like "what greater pleasure can there be than to see a stamp-man hanging on a tree."[10]

When the sun had disappeared and the better sort of the protestors had returned home, apprentices, rope workers from the shipyards, unemployed sailors, and day laborers reassembled, some fresh from a few drinks in the many taverns along King Street and its abutting alleys. Tavern keepers like John Marston joined them in the streets, in part because they were his patrons. His Golden Ball tavern welcomed thirsty "Sons of Liberty" like those who planned to continue the protest that night.[11]

The mob, now led by McIntosh in person, shifted from parading with symbolic figurines to breaking and entering houses along King Street, ripping the boards off the partially completed Oliver warehouse, and carrying them to his home, where they were burned. They pulled down his garden fence, and hearing what they thought were insults or threats from within, where Oliver's friends had gathered (he had wisely fled, hearing rumors that the real object of the mob was his person), the pillagers entered the house, broke the windows, opened casks of wine, and drank his toast. When Hutchinson and the sheriff arrived to assess the damage (and urge whomever was still on the premises to disperse), they were met with shouts of "to your arms, my boys," and a shower of stones followed, chasing the officials. The governor asked the colonel of the militia to "beat an alarm," but he replied, "as soon as the drum is heard, the drummer would be knocked down, and the drum broke, and . . . probably all of the drummers of the regiment were in the mob."[12]

On the evening of August 26, while Hutchinson was at supper with his children, a well-wisher ran up to his house and warned him that the mob was on its way. Pulled away from the defense of his home by his daughter's plea that he depart, he was not there to see the vanguard of the mob break down his door with axes. The rest of the mob surged through the house and the cellar and rushed back out into the street in search of him. He returned at four in the morning to find "one of the best finished houses in the province had nothing remaining but the bare walls and floors. Not contented with tearing off all the wainscot and hangings and splitting the doors to pieces they beat down the partition [interior] walls and although that alone cost them near two hours they cut down the cupola or lanthern and they began to take the slate and boards from the roof." They carried off his tableware, family pictures, furniture, clothing, and about £900 sterling in money. They also destroyed his books and papers, including "manuscripts . . . I had been collecting

Thomas Hutchinson (1711–1780), portrait by Edward Truman, 1741.

for 30 years besides a great number of public papers in my custody." Hutchinson was left with the clothes on his back and the kindness of his neighbors to provide for him and his family.[13]

Franklin's own home in Philadelphia nearly suffered the same fate as Hutchinson's. Franklin's house had been a target of the rioters in Philadelphia. His wife Deborah, her brother, and his friends mobilized to defend the newly finished building. Franklin heard about the tempest weeks later and wrote his wife, "I honor much the spirit and courage you showed."[14]

The Act was to go into effect on November 1, 1765, but the stamps were never used.

Colonial leaders like Virginia's Patrick Henry and Massachusetts' Samuel Adams had spoken out against the Act in the colonial assemblies that Spring. In May, Henry introduced a series of resolutions against the Act in the Virginia

House of Burgesses (assembly). His proposals were widely publicized in colonial newspapers and adopted by other legislatures.

By Summer, word of the Boston mob's actions—and the weakness of the official response—flew from colony to colony, and mobs forced stamp collector after collector to resign their posts. In the weeks between the end of active mob violence and the date the Act was due to go into effect, delegates to a Stamp Act Congress from Massachusetts, Rhode Island, Connecticut, New Jersey, Maryland, and South Carolina gathered in New York City. From October 3 to October 25, the delegates deliberated and, over a few dissents, finally drafted and dispatched a Declaration of Rights to the other legislatures and petitions to the Crown and Parliament.

The Grenville ministry had already fallen on July 10, 1765, for reasons having nothing to do with the crisis in America, and its makeshift replacement, led by Charles Watson-Wentworth, Lord Rockingham, a wealthy and well-connected member of the House of Lords who personally disliked Grenville, showed little stomach for enforcement of the Stamp Act. Rockingham conceded that the Act could not be enforced, adding to it his own belief that the stamps would injure British trade in the colonies. Pitt rose in the Commons to announce his opinion, somewhat belatedly, that the Stamp Act had been unconstitutional from its inception and should be rescinded. But Parliament passed a "Declaratory Act" in 1766 reasserting its authority to legislate for the colonies.[15]

The dialogue over the Stamp Act stretched up and down the North American coast and across the Atlantic to the metropolitan centers of power in Britain. It lasted over a year, and its ominous shadow fell over subsequent parliamentary enactments and colonial protests until the delegates to the second Continental Congress signed a Declaration of Independence. Among its indictments of imperial malfeasance was "For imposing Taxes on us without our Consent" that would later become the watchword of Whig intellectuals in America. But the centerpiece of the dialogue was Franklin's three-hour examination, and that is the centerpiece of the documents herein.

There was much in the contemporary literature of protest that had a symbolic or nonfactual character. Some historians have dismissed this often overwrought language as "propaganda" the protestors used to rouse the common people's ire or to denounce the common people when they arrayed against authority. Thus Stamp Act protesters in Boston and North Carolina royal governor William Tryon both blasted as "traitorous dogs" (animal analogies often featured in this kind of defamatory rhetoric) their opponents in the protests. Such persuasive language enabled gangs to recast themselves as Sons of Liberty and loyalists to turn colonial patriots into animals. The fact that America in 1765 was still largely a face-to-face society made such inflammatory speech particularly easy to convert into physical confrontation.[16]

Benjamin Franklin (1706–1790), portrait by Michael Deas, 2003.

While it may be true that the reading back of modern ideas of propaganda into the political controversies of the eighteenth century is inappropriate, the way in which written protests and responses worked derived in part from their origin in acts of speech. Ideas that appeared in the rich pamphlet and newspaper literature of the time began as speech. Such speech, repeated across time and place, reused and made conventional, shaped the formal discourse of parliamentary oratory and lawmaking. Many intellectual historians now think of these pronouncements as "speech-acts"—that is, they read the actions, stances, opinions, and other actual real-time events back into the words that history has recorded. That is what the following pages will attempt to do for Franklin's examination in Parliament.[17]

CHRONOLOGY

FEBRUARY 10, 1763	Treaty of Paris ends the French and Indian War, giving Britain control of much of North America east of the Mississippi but emptying the British treasury
APRIL 8, 1763	George Grenville named the head of George III's government
APRIL 5, 1764	Passage of the Sugar Act
1765	
FEBRUARY 27	Debate over the Stamp Act in Parliament
MARCH 23	Stamp Act signed into law
MAY–DECEMBER	Colonial assemblies pass resolutions asking for repeal of Stamp Act
MAY 30	Virginia House of Burgesses resolves, Patrick Henry speech
JULY 10	Grenville ministry replaced by one led by Charles Watson-Wentworth, Lord Rockingham
JULY–NOVEMBER	Anti-Stamp Act protests and riots break out in Boston, New York City, Newport (Rhode Island), Charlestown (South Carolina). and other colonial ports
OCTOBER 7–24	Stamp Act Congress, New York City, frames resolves and sends them to Parliament and the king
1766	
JANUARY–FEBRUARY	Debates in Parliament on repeal; Grenville is derided by his brother-in-law and predecessor as leader of Parliament, William Pitt
FEBRUARY 13	Benjamin Franklin examined in Parliament on the colonial response to the Stamp Act
MARCH 18	Stamp Act repealed
MARCH 23	Declaratory Act signed into law
NOVEMBER 13, 1770	Grenville dies, a revered elder statesman
JANUARY 29, 1774	Lord Wedderburn harangues Franklin in the "Cockpit" over the publication of Hutchinson's letters
APRIL 17, 1790	Franklin dies, an American icon

CHAPTER 1

A Stamp Act Is Proposed and Passed

On February 6 and 13, 1765, George Grenville explained why Parliament had the authority to pass a stamp tax. Note that the account is in the third person, the work of a listener taking notes rather than a copy of a Grenville speech. While Grenville probably had prepared notes for his address—he was a trained lawyer—he did not read a speech to the House of Commons, or at least, unlike a handful of his parliamentary contemporaries, he did not arrange for a copy of a speech to be published. One might note his aside that he wished "those who had gone before him" had marked a path for him to follow. While this may be a lawyer's way of lamenting the absence of clear precedents, it can also be read as a swipe at the Duke of Newcastle's inept and self-dealing administration of colonial affairs. Grenville and Newcastle were political enemies.[18]

Grenville's manifest purpose in proposing the legislation was to raise a revenue, but he had other, more fundamental aims in mind. Specifically, he wanted the colonies more closely tied to the economic and political needs of the home country. Also, he desired the colonists to obey the law, in this case the Navigation Acts. Finally, he insisted that the absence of formal colonial representation in Parliament could not be grounds for objections to the measure, as the colonists, like many in England, were represented "virtually" by the whole of Parliament. Behind this assertion lay the notion that members of Parliament were not merely delegates of their constituents, but trustees for the common good. As his secretary, Thomas Whately, wrote in defense of the proposed Act, "the British empire in Europe and America is still the same power" and there could only be one final source of authority for all the empire's parts—Parliament. Seen in this light, Grenville's program was not a piecemeal one but a grand (and to his thinking long overdue) attempt to reform the entire structure of empire.[19]

"He proposed taxing America from public motive. Private considerations of his own choice would have prevented him if they had been consulted. Wishes those who had gone before him had marked out a path to him which he might more easily follow. His conduct would then have been less liable to misconstruction.

"The reason of the delaying the proposal to this year was to gain all possible information and to give Americans an opportunity of conveying information to this House, whose ears are always open to receive knowledge and to act to it. The officers of the revenue have done their duty in gaining all possible knowledge of the subject.

"The objection of the colonies is from the general right of mankind not to be taxed but by their representatives. This goes to all laws in general. The Parliament of Great Britain virtually represents the whole Kingdom, not actually great trading towns. The merchants of London and the East India Company are not represented. Not a twentieth part of the people are actually represented. . . . All colonies are subject to the dominion of the mother country, whether they are a colony of the freest or the most absolute government.

"The particular propriety of this mode of raising the tax. Objection, that this tax will produce disturbance and discontent and prevent improvement among the colonies. He has no motive, he can have no motive, for taxing a colony, but that of doing his duty. But as to this objection, when will the time come when enforcing a tax will not give discontent, if this tax does produce it after what we have done and suffered for America? And therefore if we reject this proposition now, we shall declare that we ought not to tax the colonies. And we need not declare after a year's time that we ought not, for then we cannot."

The passage of the Stamp Act was not without incident, however, as colonial merchants lobbied their opposite numbers in England against it, and a few "opposition" members of Parliament weighed in with their concerns. One of the latter was Colonel Isaac Barré, a veteran of the French and Indian War and a friend to American interests. He spoke to the Commons about his concerns.

Barré knew that some kind of revenue act was necessary to deal with Britain's staggering postwar debt, but he seemed to have adopted the idea, current in the colonies, that earlier British imperial policy was one of intentional neglect. Colonial leaders would call this "salutary neglect" and argue that Britain's relatively light-handed governance of the colonies had allowed them, and the home country, to prosper. In fact, there was no such policy of salutary neglect on Britain's part. The very idea was a self-serving colonial invention. Imperial neglect was a product of inconsistent application of the Navigation Acts and the effectiveness of colonial evasion of the Navigation Acts.[20]

"The ability is not denied, but it is not proved. He believes they can pay it. His objection is that it creates disgust, I had almost said hatred. We did not plant the colonies. Most of them fled from oppression. They met with great difficulty and hardship, but as they fled from tyranny here they could not dread danger there. They flourished not by our care but by our neglect. They have increased while we did not attend to them. They shrink under our hand. . . . We are the mother country, let us be cautious not to get the name of stepmother."

Barré waxed even more eloquent when it came to defending the colonists' own exertions. His argument that the colonies were established and grew through the efforts of the colonists rather than the tender care of English officialdom was widely read by colonial protest leaders and would reappear as the centerpiece of Thomas Jefferson's much-admired (among the Revolutionaries at least) A Summary View of the Rights of British America *(1774). As Jefferson himself admitted many years later, his defense of the rebellion was based on ideas already widely held rather than from his original thinking.*

"They planted by your care? No! your oppressions planted them in America. They fled from your tyranny to a then uncultivated and unhospitable country, where they exposed themselves to almost all the hardships to which human nature is liable, and among others to the cruelties of a savage foe, the most subtle and I take upon me to say the most formidable of any people upon the face of God's Earth. And yet, actuated by the principles of true English liberty, they met all these hardships with pleasure, compared with those they suffered in their own country, from the hands of those who should have been their friends.

"They nourished up by *your* indulgence? They grew by your neglect of them: as soon as you began to care about them, that care was exercised in sending persons to rule over them, in one department and another, who were perhaps the deputies of deputies to some member of this House sent to spy out their liberty, to misrepresent their actions and to prey upon them; men whose behavior on many occasions has caused the blood of those Sons of Liberty to recoil within them; men promoted to the highest seats of justice, some, who to my knowledge were glad by going to a foreign country to escape being brought to the bar of a court of justice in their own.

"They protected by *your* arms? They have nobly taken up arms in your defense, have exerted a valour amidst their constant and laborious industry for the defense of a country, whose frontier, while drenched in blood, its interior parts have yielded all its little savings to your emolument. And believe me, remember I this day told you so, that same spirit of freedom which actuated that people at first, will accompany them still. But prudence forbids me to explain myself further."

Barré was right to be concerned: The Act was the most intrusive of all impositions, not only as a tax, but in the great variety and significance of the items taxed. In fact, the tax was easily collected, for it was to be paid on prestamped (hence the term "stamp tax") paper. The paper was to be shipped to colonial ports and distributed by collectors named for the purpose. The collectors were to profit from fees for their services, making the office a highly remunerative one. It was this kind of patronage that usually attached the interest of leading colonists to the empire. The fee system was the only form of payment royal judges, customs officers, surveyors, Indian agents, and other imperial bureaucrats in the colonies had, apart from funds voted them by the colonial assemblies. A salary system was proposed in 1773, but by that time such direct payment was highly suspect as another form of British imposition on American liberty.

THE STAMP ACT

The Stamp Act passed into law on March 23, 1765. It was comparable in form to a stamp duty that went all the way back to 1694. The earlier act had a similar motive: War between William and Mary's England and Louis XIV's France was bankrupting the English treasury. A new means of raising revenue was necessary. But the tax then, and in 1765, did not have an end date, nor was it explicitly tied to wartime exertions. Thus the 1694 tax was still imposed on Englishmen, and the colonists could expect the 1765 tax to remain in effect for the indefinite future. What was more, the tax was imposed in peacetime, not during the common exertions of wartime. The comprehensiveness of the duties, applying to all manner of public papers and many private ones, for example college degrees, was one of the more striking features of the Act. Looking it over carefully (although the text of legislative enactments can be both trying and boring to read), one can see how a broad spectrum of colonial public opinion might be aroused by this "internal tax" on everyday life in the colonies.[21]

"An Act for granting and applying certain stamp duties, and other duties, in the British colonies and plantations in America, towards further defraying the expences of defending, protecting, and securing the same; and for amending such parts of the several acts of parliament relating to the trade and revenues of the said colonies and plantations, as direct the manner of determining and recovering the penalties and forfeitures therein mentioned . . .

"[All legal papers, e.g.] For every skin or piece of vellum or parchment, or sheet or piece of paper, on which shall be engrossed, written, or printed, any declaration, plea, replication, rejoinder, demurrer or other pleading, or any copy thereof; in any court of law within the British colonies and plantations in America, a stamp duty of three pence . . .

"[All shipping documents, e.g.] For every skin or piece of vellum or parchment, or sheet or piece of paper, on which shall be engrossed, written, or printed, any note or bill of lading, which shall be signed for any kind of goods, wares, or merchandise, to be exported from, or any docket or clearance granted within the said colonies and plantations, a stamp duty of four pence . . .

"[All government documents, e.g.] For every skin or piece of vellum or parchment, or sheet or piece of paper, on which any grant, of any liberty, privilege, or franchise, under the seal or sign manual of any governor, proprietor, or public officer, alone, or in conjunction with any other person or persons, or with any council, or any council and assembly, or any exemplification of the same, shall be engrossed, written, or printed, within the said colonies and plantations, a stamp duty of six pounds . . .

"[All licenses, e.g.] For every skin or piece of vellum or parchment, or sheet or piece of paper, on which shall be engrossed, written, or printed, any license for retailing of wine, to be granted to any person who shall not take out a license for retailing of spirituous liquors, within the said colonies and plantations, a stamp duty of four pounds . . .

"[All deeds, e.g.] For every skin or piece of vellum or parchment, or sheet or piece of paper, on which shall be engrossed, written, or printed, any order or warrant for surveying or setting out any quantity of land, not exceeding one hundred acres, issued by any governor, proprietor, or any public officer, alone, or in conjunction with any other person or persons, or with any council, or any council and assembly, within the British colonies and plantations in America, a stamp duty of six pence . . .

"[All contracts, e.g.] For every skin or piece of vellum or parchment, or sheet or piece of paper, on which shall be engrossed, written, or printed, any indenture, lease, conveyance, contract, stipulation, bill of sale, charter party, protest, articles of apprenticeship or covenant (except for the hire of servants not apprentices, and also except such other matters as herein before charged) within the British colonies and plantations in America, a stamp duty of two shillings and six pence . . .

"[All cards and dice, e.g.] And for and upon every pack of playing cards, and all dice, which shall be sold or used within the said colonies and plantations . . .

"[All publications, e.g.] And for and every paper called a pamphlet, and upon every newspaper, containing public news or occurrences, which shall be printed, dispersed, and made public, within any of the said colonies and plantations, and for and upon such advertisements as are hereinafter mentioned, the respective duties following . . .

CHAPTER 2

The Stamp Act Defended and Protested, 1765

As news of the impending passage of the Act reached the colonies, colonial assemblies that were in session responded vigorously. The Virginia House of Burgesses was one of these, and although many of the members had already departed Williamsburg for home, the assembly was still in session when Patrick Henry proposed a series of resolutions. Colonial assemblies were locally elected, and among their members were local leaders like Henry. Members generally came from leading families, and although the franchise (right to vote) included nearly all property-owning males, in the 1761 election only one third of those eligible to vote actually cast their ballots. Voting was open and candidates knew who voted for whom.[22]

Henry was the son of a prosperous immigrant planter and local officeholder, and disastrous stints as a shopkeeper and bartender convinced him that his gifts lay elsewhere. He decided to read law. In 1760, after six weeks of haphazard study, Henry managed to convince his examiners that his "abysmal ignorance of the law" was offset by his natural genius for disputation. Fortunately for Henry, local law practice did not depend upon book learning, and his energy, oratorical skills, and willingness to represent anyone in any matter, added to his local status, brought him business and prosperity.

Henry had already successfully argued the Parson's Cause. Even before Grenville tried to figure how to raise a revenue in the colonies, the British bureau responsible for gathering information and formulating policy for the colonies, the Board of Trade, and the Privy Council, the king's closest advisors, were trying to rein in the long-neglected independence of colonial governments. The worst offenders in this regard were the colonial assemblies. They ignored the rule that all colonial legislation had to be approved by the Privy Council before the laws could go into effect. The most striking example of this campaign to curb the colonial legislatures came in Virginia, when the Board advised the Privy Council to set aside Virginia's "Two Penny Act" (1758). Through that act, the House of Burgesses had artificially set the price of tobacco at two pence per pound, after a drought had driven up the price to four and a half pence. The legislature had to act, because tobacco was the currency of Virginia and most debts and many public contracts allowed payment in tobacco certificates. One of those contracts set the salary for Anglican clergymen. Although others hurt by the artificially low price did not complain, the Anglican ministry sent one of their number to England to lobby for the disallowance of the act as prejudicial to the Anglican church in the colony. The board heard the petition favorably in May 1759. In August, the Privy Council concurred.

In Virginia, the ministers were elated at the news and sued their respective vestries for back pay. Unfortunately for the clergymen, the same men who served as vestrymen filled the jury box and the ministers lost their cases. Governor Dinwiddie, though instructed to aid the clergy, could do little, and one case became a cause célèbre. *For two hours on December 1, 1762, in the case of* The Reverend James Maury v. Fredericksville Parish *(known locally as the Parson's Cause), Henry harangued the jury, arguing, among other things, that if the king took away from the colonial assembly the right to legislate, he must be a tyrant. The jury found for the vestry.*

On May 30, 1765, Henry proposed the following resolutions to the House of Burgesses; five were adopted, the sixth was voted down, and the seventh was never voted on. When he left for his home, the House decided to rescind passage of the fifth. Henry incorporated the idea that all the rights that Englishmen possessed in the home country had come to the colonies. Henry was not a scholar (it was reputed that he only passed his bar examination because his examiners were his relatives), but every educated Anglo-American knew some English history, and an important part of that history was the struggle between Parliament and the Crown for control over taxation. Henry believed that Parliament's right to determine tax law translated into the colonial assemblies' exclusive right to tax or not tax the colonists. Note also that he rejected the idea of virtual representation that Grenville had asserted in defense of the Act. Whether or not Grenville was right, in fact and in law such practices in the colonies that resembled the rights of Englishmen, for example land ownership, jury trial, and holding elections for colonial assemblies, were privileges (or "liberties" as the term was used in England), not rights. The crown could rescind them at will.[23]

"Resolved, that the first adventurers and settlers of His Majesty's colony and dominion of Virginia brought with them and transmitted to their posterity, and all other His Majesty's subjects since inhabiting in this His Majesty's said colony, all the liberties, privileges, franchises, and immunities that have at any time been held, enjoyed, and possessed by the people of Great Britain.

"Resolved, that by two royal charters, granted by King James I, the colonists aforesaid are declared entitled to all liberties, privileges, and immunities of denizens and natural subjects to all intents and purposes as if they had been abiding and born within the Realm of England.

"Resolved, that the taxation of the people by themselves, or by persons chosen by themselves to represent them, who can only know what taxes the people are able to bear, or the easiest method of raising them, and must themselves be affected by every tax laid on the people, is the only security against a burdensome taxation, and the distinguishing characteristic of British freedom, without which the ancient constitution cannot exist.

"Resolved, that His Majesty's liege people of this his most ancient and loyal colony have without interruption enjoyed the inestimable right of being governed by such laws, respecting their internal policy and taxation, as are derived from their own consent, with the approbation of their sovereign, or his substitute; and that the same has never been forfeited or yielded up, but has been constantly recognized by the kings and people of Great Britain.

"Resolved, therefore that the General Assembly of this Colony have the only and exclusive Right and Power to lay Taxes and Impositions upon the inhabitants of this Colony and that every Attempt to vest such Power in any person or persons whatsoever other than the General Assembly aforesaid has a manifest Tendency to destroy British as well as American Freedom.

"Resolved, That His Majesty's liege people, the inhabitants of this Colony, are not bound to yield obedience to any law or ordinance whatever, designed to impose any taxation whatsoever upon them, other than the laws or ordinances of the General Assembly aforesaid.

"Resolved, That any person who shall, by speaking or writing, assert or maintain that any person or persons other than the General Assembly of this Colony, have any right or power to impose or lay any taxation on the people here, shall be deemed an enemy to His Majesty's Colony."

When challenged by one of the more conservative members of the lower house, Henry was reported by one observer to have uttered the now-famous words, "if this be treason, make the most of it"—but that may not have been what he said at all. At any rate, Virginia's royal lieutenant governor Francis Fauquier (the governor was Jeffery Amherst, former commander in chief of royal forces in America during the French and Indian War who now resided in England) wrote an account of the debates on the resolves to his superiors in England. In mitigating his failure to control the burgesses (he did not chair the assembly and only knew of its deliberations the next day), he stressed that the

resolutions came at the very end of the session, when but 39 of the 116 delegates were still attending.[24]

"In the course of the debates I have heard that very indecent language was used by a Mr. Henry a young lawyer who had not been a month a member of the House; who carried all the young members with him; so that I hope I am authorised in saying there is cause at least to doubt whether this would have been the sense of the colony if more their representatives had done their duty by attending to the end of the session."

Newspapers in the colonies reported the Henry Resolutions of May 30 (with the strong language of the final three resolves included) as if the House of Burgesses had actually passed all seven of them, and various mainland colonial legislatures adopted similar language. Typical was the final article that the Rhode Island assembly adopted on September 15, 1765.[25]

"That all the officers in this colony, appointed by the authority thereof, be, and they are hereby directed, to proceed in the execution of their respective offices, in the same manner as usual, and that this assembly will indemnify and save harmless all the said officers, on account of their conduct, agreeable to this resolution . . . That his majesty's liege people, the inhabitants of this colony, are not bound to yield obedience to any law or ordinance, designed to impose any internal taxation whatsoever on them, other than the laws or ordinances of the general assembly aforesaid."

Some leading American politicians, like Pennsylvania's Joseph Galloway, defended the legality of the Stamp Act and urged objections to it be cast as respectful petitions to the better nature of Parliament. While in the colonies, the tax was hated as an "internal tax," designed to raise revenue, as opposed to an "external tax" (customs duties, for example, which were intended to regulate trade and pay for the customs collection rather than raise additional revenue), Galloway, a lawyer, knew that such taxes were long levied in England. Indeed, personal taxes on the wealthy; the hearth tax, a type of real estate tax based on the number of chimneys a house had; and stamped paper taxes were all in place in England by the end of the seventeenth century.

Galloway was an ally of Franklin in colonial politics and no friend to the Grenvillites in Parliament. Nevertheless, he took pride in the empire and his English heritage, and he tried to be realistic and conciliatory, a voice of reason against the swelling tide of protest. Galloway would be a voice of moderation at the Stamp Act Congress and in 1774 at the first meeting of the Continental Congress. When the Revolutionary War came, he sided with the British, sailed to England in 1778, and never returned to America. He died in 1803.

Galloway published his opinions in the form of a letter to the editor of a pro-British newspaper in New York City.[26]

"At a time when *almost every American pen* is employed in placing the transactions of the Parliament of our mother country is the *most odious light*, and in *alienating the affections* of a numerous and loyal people *from the royal person* of the best of sovereigns; permit [me], however unpopular the task, through the impartial channel of your paper, to point out the impudence and folly of such conduct, and to give a brief and true state of the facts included in the dispute between Great Britain and her colonies. From whence the cool and unprejudiced may form a right judgment of the motives of her late [recent] conduct, and of the impropriety and rashness of the method that is taken to prevail on her to alter or repeal her measures.

"It is a truth too universally known that the people of England are involved in a debt under which they struggle with the utmost difficulty. From its enormity many judicious persons have predicted the ruin of the nation. Foreign powers rely on it as the only foundation of their hopes of reducing the British dominions. The protection of America has, in no small degree, contributed to this burden of the mother country. To the large sums of money that have been expended from the English treasury and the parental care of a British Parliament, we in a great measure owe our present freedom from Indian barbarities, popish cruelties and superstition. . . .

"The preservation of America is of the utmost importance to Great Britain. A loss of it to the British crown would greatly diminish its strength, and the possession of it to any other nation would give an increase of wealth and power totally inconsistent with the safety of Britons. *If* then the power of protection is rightfully and solely vested in the crown; *If* America is of so much importance to her mother country; and *if* it is just and reasonable that she should contribute towards her own defense, so essential to her own and the happiness of Great Britain, *will any be so absurd as to deny the* reasonableness, *the* necessity, *of the crown's having some* certainty *that she will pay her proportion of aids when requisite and* demanded. . . .

"It is a proof of the greatest infatuation [delusion] to conceive that we can bully the British nation, now at peace with the whole world, and possessed of strength which the united powers of France and Spain could not subdue. Let us then convert our idle threats into dutiful remonstrances [petitions]. Reveal to them the poverty of our circumstances, and rectify the false representations which they have received of our wealth. Show them our incapacity to pay the impositions which they have laid upon us without more freedom of commerce and a circulating medium to carry on that commerce. Tell them that, should they make a thousand acts of Parliament to oblige us, we cannot give what we have not, and what they prevent us from procuring for want [need] of a due attention to our circumstances. And tell them our incapacity to pay the debt already due to the British merchants, our inability to take off [trade in] their future manufactures, and the impossibility of our contributing to the wealth, power and glory of our mother country, unless she will relax her present measures, which so essentially affect her own as well as our welfare."

In the fall of 1765, nine colonies sent delegates to New York City at the behest of the Massachusetts Bay Colony to discuss a common response to the Stamp Act. The delegates to the Stamp Act Congress met from October 7 to October 25, with the various colonial assemblies' protests in hand. There was no basis in the colonial charters or the various acts of Parliament for such a congress, but it had a precedent in the Albany Congress of 1754. Although the resolves of that gathering (prepared by Franklin) to create a kind of colonial confederation were universally rejected by the colonial assemblies, the resolves of the Stamp Act Congress were welcomed by the colonial assemblies. Though its deliberations were secret, the identity of the delegates was not. Among them were well-known opponents of Parliament like lawyers James Otis Jr. of Massachusetts and John Dickinson of Pennsylvania, and future revolutionary leaders like Robert R. Livingston of New York, Thomas McKean of Pennsylvania, and Caesar Rodney of Delaware.

The Congress's "Declaration of Rights and Grievances," in the form of a petition, was the work of Dickinson, who would soon explain the argument in the Declaration at greater length in his "Letters from a Pennsylvania Farmer." For the present, the document, signed by thirteen delegates representing six of the nine colonies present (Massachusetts, Maryland, Pennsylvania, New Jersey, Rhode Island, and New York) and approved by all but one of the thirteen mainland colonies, was sent to the king and to both houses of Parliament.[27]

"The Members of this Congress, sincerely devoted, with the warmest Sentiments of Affection and Duty to his Majesty's Person and Government, inviolably attached to the present happy Establishment of the Protestant Succession, and with Minds deeply impressed by a Sense of the present and impending Misfortunes of the British Colonies on this Continent; having considered as maturely as Time will permit, the Circumstances of the said Colonies, esteem it our indispensable Duty, to make the following Declarations of our humble Opinion, respecting the most Essential Rights and Liberties of the Colonists, and of the Grievances under which they labour, by Reason of several late Acts of Parliament . . . his Majesty's Liege Subjects in these Colonies, are entitled to all the inherent Rights and Liberties of his Natural born Subjects, within the Kingdom of Great-Britain. . . . It is inseparably essential to the Freedom of a People, and the undoubted Right of Englishmen, that no Taxes be imposed on them, but with their own Consent, given personally, or by their Representatives. . . . The only Representatives of the People of these Colonies, are Persons chosen therein by themselves, and that no Taxes ever have been, or can be Constitutionally imposed on them, but by their respective Legislature . . . the late Act of Parliament, entitled, An Act for granting and applying certain Stamp Duties, and other Duties, in the British Colonies and Plantations in America, &c. by imposing Taxes on the Inhabitants of these Colonies, and the said Act, and several other Acts, by extending the Jurisdiction of the Courts of Admiralty beyond its ancient Limits, have a manifest Tendency to subvert the Rights and Liberties of the Colonists . . . and that the Duties [a reference to the Sugar Act] imposed by several late Acts of Parliament, from the peculiar Circumstances of these Colonies, will be extremely Burthensome and Grievous; and from the scarcity of Specie, the Payment of them absolutely impracticable.

"Lastly, That it is the indispensable Duty of these Colonies, to the best of Sovereigns, to the Mother Country, and to themselves, to endeavour by a loyal and dutiful Address to his Majesty, and humble Applications to both Houses of Parliament, to procure the Repeal of the Act for granting and applying certain Stamp Duties, of all Clauses of any other Acts of Parliament, whereby the Jurisdiction of the Admiralty is extended as aforesaid, and of the other late Acts for the Restriction of American Commerce."

John Dickinson was a reluctant revolutionary. One of the most successful lawyers in Pennsylvania and Delaware, he did not vote for independence but supported it, helping to draft the Articles of Confederation, raising and leading troops in the war, later playing a major role promoting the abolition of slavery in Pennsylvania and Delaware and drafting the federal constitution. He died in the same year as Galloway.

Dickinson's pen was active in the protests against the Stamp Act, as this Pennsylvania broadside amply demonstrated. Though it had no date, from internal evidence it was printed after November 1, 1765, when the stamps were to be distributed. Note Dickinson's professions of loyalty to Britain and the crown, even as he extolled the protest. Dickinson would in 1767 draft "Letters from a Pennsylvania Farmer" denouncing all taxation without representation.[28]

"The critical time is now come, when you are reduced to the necessity of forming a resolution, upon a point of the most alarming instance that can engage the attention of men. Your conduct at this period must decide the future fortunes of yourselves and your posterity. You must decide whether Pennsylvanians from henceforward, shall be freemen or slaves . . .

"We have seen the day on which an act of Parliament, imposing stamp duties on the British colonies in America, was appointed to take effect, and we have seen the inhabitants of these colonies with an unexampled unanimity compelling the stamp-officers throughout the provinces to resign their employments. The virtuous indignation with which they [the colonists] have acted, was inspired by the generous love of liberty, and guided by a sense of loyalty to the best of kings, and of duty to the mother country."

Massachusetts lawyer and politician John Adams had no small part in the Boston-area protests. Though conservative by nature and ideology, he viewed the protests as a vindication of existing American rights rather than the opening act of a new kind of popular politics. In 1774 he would attend the first Continental Congress and begin a campaign for independence from Britain. He was a member of the committee that drafted the Declaration of Independence, a diplomat, the country's first vice president and second president, and one of its most honored elder statesmen. He died on July 4, 1826.

As 1765 came to a close, Adams wrote about the meaning of the protests and their likely effect on political events to come.[29]

"The Year 1765 has been the most remarkable Year of my Life. That enormous Engine, fabricated by the British Parliament, for battering down all the Rights and Liberties of America, I mean the Stamp Act, has raised and spread, thro the whole Continent, a Spirit that will be recorded to our Honour, with all future Generations. In every Colony, from Georgia to New Hampshire inclusively, the Stamp Distributors and Inspectors have been compelled, by the unconquerable Rage of the People, to renounce their offices. Such and so universal has been the Resentment of the People, that every Man who has dared to speak in favour of the Stamps, or to soften the detestation in which they are held, how great soever his Abilities and Virtues had been esteemed before, or whatever his fortune, Connections and Influence had been, has been seen to sink into universal Contempt and Ignominy.

"The People, even to the lowest Ranks, have become more attentive to their Liberties, more inquisitive about them, and more determined to defend them, than they were ever before known or had occasion to be. Innumerable have been the Monuments of Wit, Humour, Sense, Learning, Spirit, Patriotism, and Heroism, erected in the several Colonies and Provinces, in the Course of this Year. Our Presses have groaned, our Pulpits have thundered, our Legislatures have resolved, our Towns have voted, The Crown Officers have every where trembled, and all their little Tools and Creatures, been afraid to Speak and ashamed to be seen.

"This Spirit however has not yet been sufficient to banish, from Persons in Authority, that Timidity, which they have discovered from the Beginning. The executive Courts have not yet dared to adjudge the Stamp-Act void nor to proceed with Business as usual, tho it should seem that Necessity alone would be sufficient to justify Business, at present, tho the Act should be allowed to be obligatory.

"The Stamps are in the Castle [i.e. on Castle Island in Boston Harbor]. Mr. [Andrew] Oliver has no Commission. The Governor has no Authority to distribute, or even to unpack the Bales, the Act has never been proclaimed nor read in the Province; Yet the Probate office is shut, the Custom House is shut, the Courts of justice are shut, and all Business seems at a Stand. Yesterday and the day before, the two last days of Service for January Term, only one Man asked me for a Writ [to begin a law suit], and he was soon determined to waive his Request. I have not drawn a Writ since 1st. Novr.

"How long We are to remain in this languid Condition, this passive Obedience to the Stamp Act, is not certain. But such a Pause cannot be lasting. Debtors grow insolent. Creditors grow angry. And it is to be expected that the Public offices will very soon be forced open, unless such favourable Accounts should be received from England, as to draw away the Fears of the Great, or unless a greater Dread of the Multitude should drive away the Fear of Censure from G. Britain."

The British press printed a number of pieces on the colonial response to the Act. Most supported the government (not surprising, as criticism of the government in the press was the serious crime of seditious libel). Some of these were as virulent as the colonial protests themselves. The targets of the letter are easily identified as Virginia and Massachusetts political leaders.[30]

"The Virginians indeed are immersed in libertinism, and the New-Englanders swell with the stiff tenets of independency. The latter are a crabbed race, not very unlike their half brothers, the Indians, for unsocial principles, and an unrelenting cruelty . . . Shall Britain yield up her birth rights, for the sake of pleasing the whim of Virginians, whose emaciated bodies and pale faces, prove at first sight the degeneracy of their morals, and the consumptive state of their natural constitutions. These yellow shadows of men are by no means fit for a conflict with our troops . . . As for the New-Englanders, I have given their characters already. They are the joke of America . . . Their valor arising from the streams of their poisonous rum, will quickly evaporate in sudden tumults . . . The idea of a rebellion in America, in consequence of such an unimportant subject of dispute, is merely chimerical."

CHAPTER 3

The Debate on Repeal Begins, 1766

Although no longer first minister in His Majesty's government, Grenville was still a member of Parliament, and he defended the Act and his actions on the floor of the House of Commons on January 14, 1766. His tone was belligerent, but he must have sensed that repeal was a foregone conclusion.[31]

"This kingdom has the sovereign, the supreme legislative power over America, is granted. It cannot be denied; and taxation is a part of that sovereign power. It is one branch of the legislation. It is, it has been exercised, over those who are not, who were never represented. It is exercised over the India Company, the merchants of London, and the proprietors of the stocks, and over great manufacturing towns. It was exercised over the county . . . of Chester . . . before they sent any representatives to parliament. . . . Protection and obedience are reciprocal. Great Britain protects America, America is bound to yield obedience. If not, tell me when the Americans were emancipated? When they want the protection of this kingdom, they are always very ready to ask it. That protection has always been afforded them in the most full and ample manner. The nation has run itself into an immense debt to give them this protection; and now they are called upon to contribute a small share towards the public expense."

On the same day, William Pitt replied to Grenville in Parliament, but his defense of the colonies did not go as far as the ideas expressed in the Stamp Act Congress resolves. He also took the opportunity to defend his conduct of the war and explain how Britain benefited from it.

"I have been charged with giving birth to sedition in America. They have spoken their sentiments with freedom against this unhappy act, and that freedom has become their crime.

"Sorry I am to hear the liberty of speech in this House, imputed as a crime. No gentleman ought to be afraid to exercise it. It is a liberty by which the gentleman who calumniates it might have profited, by which he ought to have profited. He ought to have desisted from this project.

"The gentleman tells us, America is obstinate; America is almost in open rebellion. I rejoice that America has resisted. Three million of people so dead to all feelings of liberty, as voluntarily to submit to be slaves, would have been fit instruments to make slaves of the rest.

"I am no courtier of America; I stand up for this kingdom. I maintain, that the parliament has a right to bind, to restrain America. Our legislative power over the colonies is sovereign and supreme. When it ceases to be sovereign and supreme, I would advise every gentleman to sell his lands, if he can, and embark for that country.

"When two countries are connected together, like England and her colonies, without being incorporated, the one must necessarily govern; the greater must rule the less; but so rule it, as not to contradict the fundamental principles that are common to both.

"If the gentleman does not understand the difference between external and internal taxes, I cannot help it; but there is a plain distinction between taxes levied for the purpose of raising a revenue, and duties imposed for the regulation of trade, for the accommodation of the subject; although, in the consequences, some revenue might incidentally arise from the latter."

Here the debate might have rested, major figures having spoken their piece. But another major figure in the story was close at hand, and he was ready to take part in the public debate. That figure was Franklin.

CHAPTER 4

The Examination of Benjamin Franklin in Parliament, February 13, 1766

The dialogue over the Stamp Act, the first act in widespread colonial resistance to Parliament, showed how swiftly public opinion in the colonies could be marshaled and how inherently fragile was political obedience in the peripheries of the greatest empire of its day. The Atlantic, having become a highway of commerce in staple goods, slaves, and travelers, was still an obstacle to firm royal control of colonial conduct. These facets of the protest surprised members of Parliament, and they turned to the one colonist most familiar to them and widely respected, to explain what had happened and what the colonists wanted.

In 1765 Franklin was the agent for the colony of Pennsylvania, an unofficial post created by the colony's assembly to represent its interests in Parliament (and a studied offense to the proprietor, Thomas Penn, who cordially hated Franklin). Much respected in England for his experiments in electricity and for his literary and entrepreneurial talents, he was in some sense the epitome of the successes of provincialism. Although the post he held, of agent for his colony, was entirely outside of the framework of official imperial governance, Franklin was sufficiently respected to be summoned to Parliament to explain why the colonies had erupted in violent protest against the Stamp Act of 1765. He had played something of a double agent's game in the protests against the Act, at first opposing it, then recommending a friend for the post of Pennsylvania stamped paper distributor, then spurring protest in the colonies through his newspaper contacts, all the while publicly advising members of Parliament on colonial attitudes.[32]

Franklin spoke to Parliament at a critical moment in a nearly century-old Western European inquiry into the nature of government. So-called Enlightenment political philosophers like John Locke, David Hume, Montesquieu, and Voltaire debated how good government could combine traditional and popular sources of authority. The Enlightenment did not anticipate the end of old forms of government, particularly monarchy; that ideological innovation belonged to the Age of Revolution beginning in America and spreading to the Continent in the last quarter of the eighteenth century. But Enlightenment reformers saw old forms of government and the economy in a new light illuminated by the concept of enlightened self-interest.[33]

Even the most enlightened monarchies could not exist without raising revenue. The raising of necessary funds was, however, never popular among the subjects of the crown. To finance its own operation and to protect its empire at sea and on land, the British government had imposed a heavy tax load on Britons. There were duties on imports, taxes on hearths, excise taxes on goods for sale, and most intrusively stamp taxes. In the eighteenth century, one defense of these taxes was that they were in the self-interest of the taxed. Government provided essential services that benefited everyone, and the general interest should supersede individual self-interest. The reciprocal privilege government owed the taxed individual was the right to vote—representation in Parliament. Franklin and other colonial leaders had urged this on the imperial government for years.[34]

On February 13, 1766, with the stamps on their way back to England or rotting in ships' holds in colonial harbors, Franklin stood in the well of the House of Commons and for four hours withstood a barrage of questions about the reception of the Stamp Act in the colonies, particularly Massachusetts. Some of the questions were genuine attempts to understand what had gone wrong. Other questions were frankly hostile, Franklin serving as a proxy for the rebellious colonists. But Franklin was not regarded as sympathetic to the riots, and in truth he could not be held responsible for them. Members of Parliament knew that Franklin's house had been a target of the rioters in Philadelphia. Indeed, when Franklin heard about the tempest weeks later he wrote his wife, "I honor much the spirit and courage you showed."[35]

Grenville was one of the hostile interrogators. Charles Watson-Wentworth, the Marquis of Rockingham, was now the leader of the government, was well disposed toward Franklin. Pitt was also there and would have asked supportive questions, as much to embarrass Grenville as to help Franklin. He would need all the help he could get, for Franklin already had gout, and standing for so many hours, craning his neck, and cupping his ear, must have required immense physical fortitude. Franklin's own regimen of diet, exercise, and self-discipline here stood him in good stead.[36]

Although they know everyone who was a member of Parliament that day, historians will never know exactly who asked what of Franklin. The members of the House of Commons were meeting for the period February 11 to 13 as a committee of the whole, a form of session dating back to the middle of the seventeenth century ordinarily formed after the second reading of a bill (in this case the repeal of the Stamp Act). The rules of the House (now codified as Robert's Rules of Order) were modified and relaxed in the committee of the whole, in particular allowing any member to speak more than once. The

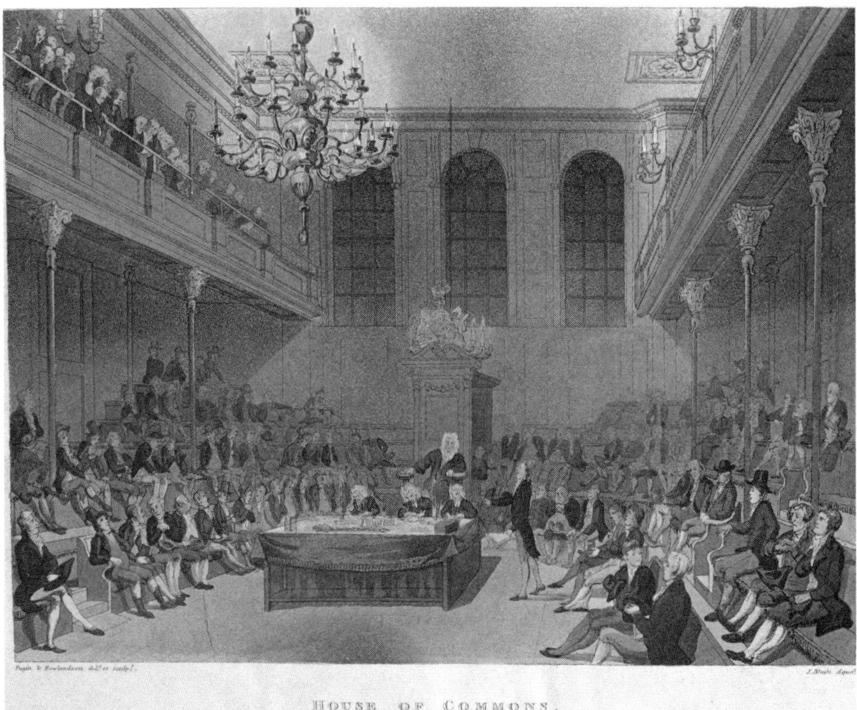

Augustus Pugin and Thomas Rowlandson, "House of Commons in 1808," Microcosm of London (1808). Fire gutted the chamber in 1834 after wooden "tally sticks" stored in the medieval Westminster palace were incinerated in the House of Lords' coal furnaces, the heat melting the copper flues and setting the entire parliamentary complex afire.

Speaker of the House does not preside, and the members act as if they were a deliberative body rather than an investigatory one. In any case, most of the questions were likely scripted by the new government and Franklin probably knew in advance and in general what they would be—after all, he had worked assiduously behind the scenes to convince Parliament to repeal the Stamp Act. One observer, the famous London evangelical preacher George Whitefield, watching from perhaps as close as the visitors' gallery, appreciated Franklin's performance. The two men were longtime friends, Franklin publishing Whitefield's journals. Whitefield later wrote that "Dr. Franklin has gained immortal honor by his behaviour at the bar of the House. His answer was always found equal to the questioner. He stood unappalled, gave pleasure to his friends, and did honour to his country."[37]

Whitefield, who had tried for many years to convert Franklin, knew that Franklin was no angel. Though he had become an icon of republican virtue by the time of his death, in life he was ambitious, sometimes unscrupulous, capable of great self-promotion, and a fierce adversary when aroused. As with the

Stamp Act, he could change his stance, cover his tracks, and hide his true motives with genial aplomb. His writings were calculated to persuade, not to reveal his true feelings, though if one lined them end to end, as modern scholars can, something of the complex man behind the mask comes into focus.

Parliament's (relatively) newfound reliance on expert testimony gave the event a modern feel, even without the C-SPAN and Twitter coverage one expects today. Franklin was asked to attend as an expert on American public opinion. Choosing Franklin as the expert made sense: Not only was he respected for his writings and his scientific achievements, he was the Postmaster General of the colonies. In this office, Franklin had his fingers on and in all manner of colonial matters. From his experience at the Albany conference, he knew leaders of other colonies and had thought about intercolonial cooperation. He read other colonial newspapers, occasionally borrowing from them to fill the pages of his own Pennsylvania Gazette. *He was a veteran newspaperman, with a circle of friendly publishers, including his own Philadelphia partner David Hall, and London printers like William Strahan, all of them ready to mold his words to appeal to public opinion. Franklin himself was a public intellectual capable of doing his own publicity, writing letters to newspapers in the home country and the colonies: "I hope . . . to see prudent measures taken by our rulers such as may heal and not widen our breaches." In fact, one of Franklin's most successful propaganda efforts was restraining colonial editors' outrage at having to use stamped paper.*[38]

What was remarkable in his appearance before the members of the House of Commons was not their choice of him, then, but, first, their apparent reliance on his expertise, or any expertise for that matter. The increasing reliance on industrial production in the economy of Britain, the rising authority of scientific knowledge, and the emergence of civil and mechanical engineering as professions all raised the visibility and importance of expertise. Experts were an increasingly common presence in English courts of law, testifying on their own knowledge about public works and private ventures.[39]

The concern for public opinion that one can see in the questions was just as important as Franklin's expertise to the members. Public opinion was certainly not the basis by which the members of the House of Commons were chosen. That body, in theory the voice of the people, was in fact hardly representative of the English people. Only propertied adult male subjects of the king could vote, and before one voted, one had to profess loyalty to the crown and acceptance of Protestant teachings. That left out over ninety percent of the adult male population. The rest were represented virtually, the members of the lower house acting as trustees for the good of the whole—at least in theory. In fact, legislative politics was riven with corruption, the king buying up votes and various leading politicians routinely using their offices for profit and their patronage to repay political favors. The most appalling form of corruption was the maldistribution of seats in the House: One largely uninhabited corner of the realm sent two members to the House of Commons while Middlesex County, with a population of nearly one million, sent only eight men.[40]

But public opinion was finding its way into the great hall at Westminster where the Commons sat. Newspapers covered the debates. Members of Parliament gave newspapers copies of their speeches. Members also read the newspapers. Some members tried to "spin" the newspaper accounts, including getting editors to change the account of parliamentary activities. Perhaps even more indicative of the changing climate of politics, some editors were able to tell members of Parliament what they must say and do. To be sure, those out of Parliament had to be careful in how they tried to orchestrate public opinion, but such arrangements were more and more common as the eighteenth century wore on, and Franklin, as we have seen, rode the crest of that wave.[41]

The questions asked Franklin hinted that many in the House of Commons recognized that public opinion in the colonies was essential to the success of any legislative program. In most of the colonies by 1765, just about all white males who paid taxes, owned property, or served in the militia could vote. Proportionally, many more colonists could vote for their legislators than Englishmen could vote for members of the House of Commons. In many of the colonies, voter deference to local elites determined who won contests for the assembly, but as the Stamp Act riots demonstrated, elite status did not matter when the public was aroused. Ordinary men could lead the mob and men of property and standing could be its victims. As well, the flood of petitions from the colonies against the Stamp Act and the resolves of the extralegal Stamp Act Congress that met in New York City in October 1765 showed that colonial public opinion could be marshaled against acts of Parliament with surprising ease and effectiveness. Parliament had received and rejected these petitions in 1765, and perhaps as the members gathered to hear Franklin, they regretted their haste.[42]

Franklin's examination came on the third day of the committee of the whole's sitting. In the gallery listened other witnesses, including colonial merchants, agents, and Franklin's friends. Although at the time the deliberations were not to be published, the clerk of the body, Thomas Tyrwhitt, had agreed to send copies of his notes to William Strahan, who arranged (at Franklin's request) for an American publication. Nathaniel Ryder, the clerk's assistant, had also taken notes, and the manuscript of these survives. David Hall, a printer, had a copy of the notes but did not rush to publish them until September, and then only in Philadelphia (to avert prosecution for violating the law against publication), omitting the names of the members who asked the questions. The printed copy soon found its way back to London, and magazines there published excerpts from the Hall version, taking care to praise the members for their precision and Franklin for his character and abilities. In short, it was a love fest, with Franklin the object of the printers' adoration. After all, he was one of them and used his office as postmaster to favor those with whom he had good relations and disfavor those with whom he had rivalries. Franklin was a tough-minded businessman in this respect.

The editors of the Papers of Benjamin Franklin *were able to assemble both manuscript and printed versions and published Franklin's own copy interleaved with the Ryder notes. The resulting account of the hearing had a twist characteristic of all of Franklin's writings. By laying the very terse questions of the members of the House of Commons alongside his longer, fuller answers, he gave the impression to the reader that he was lecturing the legislators rather than being interrogated.*[43]

One further note: The Q and A bears the unmistakable character of a concordance—that is, a conversation with the "ums" and "ers" deleted. A reading of the entire examination takes a little under an hour, but Franklin spent nearly three hours in the well of the House of Commons. One must conclude that the questions were surely not as crisp as they appear in the printed version, nor were the answers as succinct. What is more, there must have been pauses between questions and answers, as the querists framed their questions and Franklin thought about his answers. Some of the questions would have been indistinct, and some of the answers not loud enough for the entire body to hear. Thus there would have been repetitions. Although the colloquy was scripted in a larger sense, the order of the questions and the tone of voice used to pose them could not have been rehearsed. One cannot tell whether this cleanup took place at the time, as the exchange was being recorded, or later, when (like a clerk of a court) the clerk of the House produced a clean version from rough notes. The important point is that the exchange was cleaned to make the back-and-forth sharper and more useful for Franklin's purposes.

Franklin's copy numbered the questions from 1 to 174 for his own use. I have kept the numbers and added breaks, with commentary, for the purposes of this book. There is no certain way to determine who among the members asked which of the questions. Friends to the American cause in attendance that day included Rockingham and his younger protégé Edmund Burke, former prime minister William Pitt, and Isaac Barré. Grenville was also there and either asked or prompted more attacking questions.[44]

The first questions would have been asked by Rockingham himself, as he had invited Franklin to Parliament and he was the king's first minister and head of the government. They are friendly in tone, establishing the inconvenience of the tax and hinting at its unfairness. As such, they took a slap at Grenville's administration.

"[1] Q. What is your name, and place of abode?

A. Franklin, of Philadelphia.

[2] Q. Do the Americans pay any considerable taxes among themselves?

A. Certainly many, and very heavy taxes.

[3] Q. What are the present taxes in Pennsylvania, laid by the laws of the colony?

A. There are taxes on all estates real and personal, a poll tax, a tax on all offices, professions, trades and businesses, according to their profits; an excise on all wine, rum, and other spirits; and a duty of Ten Pounds per head on all Negroes imported, with some other duties."

The poll tax was introduced in early modern England to pay for its wars, falling most heavily on the wealthy nobility. It was used in some of the colonies as the basis for voting rights, as many (but not all of the colonies) tied the right to vote to property holding. Although the colonial franchise was restricted by this requirement, a far greater proportion of white males could vote in the colonies than could in England. As in England, however, women, servants, Catholics, and in the colonies, Indians, slaves, and youths could not vote.[45]

"[4] Q. For what purposes are those taxes laid?

A. For the support of the civil and military establishments of the country, and to discharge the heavy debt contracted in the last war.

[5] Q. How long are those taxes to continue?

A. Those for discharging the debt are to continue till 1772, and longer, if the debt should not be then all discharged. The others must always continue.

[6] Q. Was it not expected that the debt would have been sooner discharged?

A. It was, when the peace was made with France and Spain—But a fresh war breaking out with the Indians, a fresh load of debt was incurred, and the taxes, of course, continued longer by a new law."

The "fresh war" was an uprising by the Ohio Valley and Great Lakes Indian peoples, later called "Pontiac's Rebellion" after the Ottawa war chief who was

one of its instigators. The French allies of the Indians had treated them far more fairly than the English and the Anglo-American colonists, and when the French and Indian War ended with Canada and the trans-Appalachian West switched from French to British dominion, an alliance of Indians tried to drive the British and the colonists out of their new possessions. Franklin was no friend to the Indians, looking down on native customs and denouncing Indians as savages.[46]

"[7] Q. Are not all the people very able to pay those taxes?

A. No. The frontier counties, all along the continent, having been frequently ravaged by the enemy, and greatly impoverished, are able to pay very little tax. And therefore, in consideration of their distresses, our late tax laws do expressly favour those counties, excusing the sufferers; and I suppose the same is done in other governments.

[8] Q. Are not you concerned in the management of the Post-Office in America?

A. Yes. I am Deputy Post-Master General of North-America.

[9] Q. Don't you think the distribution of stamps, by post, to all the inhabitants, very practicable, if there was no opposition?

A. The posts only go along the sea coasts; they do not, except in a few instances, go back into the country; and if they did, sending for stamps by post would occasion an expence of postage, amounting, in many cases, to much more than that of the stamps themselves.

[10] Q. Are you acquainted with Newfoundland?

A. I never was there.

[11] Q. Do you know whether there are any post roads on that island?

A. I have heard that there are no roads at all; but that the communication between one settlement and another is by sea only.

[12] Q. Can you disperse the stamps by post in Canada?

A. There is only a post between Montreal and Quebec. The inhabitants live so scattered and remote from each other, in that vast country, that posts cannot be supported among them, and therefore they cannot get stamps per post. The English Colonies too, along the frontiers, are very thinly settled.

[13] Q. From the thinness of the back settlements, would not the stamp-act be extremely inconvenient to the inhabitants, if executed?

A. To be sure it would; as many of the inhabitants could not get stamps when they had occasion for them, without taking long journeys, and spending perhaps Three or Four Pounds, that the Crown might get Sixpence."

The next questions were Grenville's, again protocol dictating that the former prime minister have his innings. He knew that the Act would not be sustained, but thought that it, and his reputation, could be defended. Although posed in question form, Grenville's contributions lectured Franklin on the reasons why the Act could have worked.

"[14] Q. Are not the Colonies, from their circumstances, very able to pay the stamp duty?

A. In my opinion, there is not gold and silver enough in the Colonies to pay the stamp duty for one year.

[15] Q. Don't you know that the money arising from the stamps was all to be laid out in America?

A. I know it is appropriated by the act to the American service; but it will be spent in the conquered Colonies, where the soldiers are, not in the Colonies that pay it.

[16] Q. Is there not a ballance of trade due from the Colonies where the troops are posted, that will bring back the money to the old colonies?

A. I think not. I believe very little would come back. I know of no trade likely to bring it back. I think it would come from the Colonies where it was spent directly to England; for I have always observed, that in every Colony the more plenty the means of remittance to England, the more goods are sent for, and the more trade with England carried on."

The next set of questions suggested a military interest and harkened back to the period of the French and Indian War, the military capacity of the colonies, and certain diplomatic matters. The questions might have been posed by

Henry Conway, a former British general and member of Parliament who strongly supported Rockingham. Conway did not have direct experience of the colonies, but, at the time of the repeal debate serving as Secretary of State for the Southern Department, the chief administrative officer for oversight of the American colonies in the government, he might have seen this as the occasion to find out more about the colonies in his charge.

It is also possible that these questions came from William Pitt, the "great commoner." As an active participant in the debates over the previous two days, he might have decided to let Franklin's answers reiterate the points he himself had made on Tuesday and Wednesday, February 11 and 12. He too was a former prime minister, and that would have permitted him to claim to be the third questioner.

Whichever man asked them, the questions also hint at the demographic and commercial growth of the colonies, reminding the members of how important the colonists' loyalty to the empire was, a point that both Conway and Pitt had repeatedly made.[47]

"[17] Q. What number of white inhabitants do you think there are in Pennsylvania?

A. I suppose there may be about 160,000.

[18] Q. What number of them are Quakers?

A. Perhaps a third.

[19] Q. What number of Germans?

A. Perhaps another third; but I cannot speak with certainty.

[20] Q. Have any number of the Germans seen service, as soldiers, in Europe?

A. Yes,—many of them, both in Europe and America.

[21] Q. Are they as much dissatisfied with the stamp duty as the English?

A. Yes, and more; and with reason, as their stamps are, in many cases, to be double.

[22] Q. How many white men do you suppose there are in North-America?

A. About 300,000, from sixteen to sixty years of age.

[23] Q. What may be the amount of one year's imports into Pennsylvania from Britain?

A. I have been informed that our merchants compute the imports from Britain to be above 500,000 Pounds.

[24] Q. What may be the amount of the produce of your province exported to Britain?

A. It must be small, as we produce little that is wanted in Britain. I suppose it cannot exceed 40,000 Pounds.

[25] Q. How then do you pay the ballance?

A. The ballance is paid by our produce carried to the West-Indies, and sold in our own islands, or to the French, Spaniards, Danes and Dutch; by the same carried to other colonies in North-America, as to New-England, Nova-Scotia, Newfoundland, Carolina and Georgia; by the same carried to different parts of Europe, as Spain, Portugal and Italy. In all which places we receive either money, bills of exchange, or commodities that suit for remittance to Britain; which, together with all the profits on the industry of our merchants and mariners, arising in those circuitous voyages, and the freights made by their ships, center finally in Britain, to discharge the ballance, and pay for British manufactures continually used in the province, or sold to foreigners by our traders.

[26] Q. Have you heard of any difficulties lately laid on the Spanish trade?

A. Yes, I have heard that it has been greatly obstructed by some new regulations, and by the English men of war and cutters stationed all along the coast in America."

With Franklin taking a direct swipe at the Sugar Act's regulation of colonial trade, Grenville might have felt obligated to fire off a second barrage of questions at Franklin. Grenville also took the opportunity to display his knowledge of finance.

"[27] Q. Do you think it right that America should be protected by this country, and pay no part of the expence?

A. That is not the case. The Colonies raised, cloathed and paid, during the last war, near 25000 men, and spent many millions.

[28] Q. Were you not reimbursed by parliament?

A. We were only reimbursed what, in your opinion, we had advanced beyond our proportion, or beyond what might reasonably be expected from us; and it was a very small part of what we spent. Pennsylvania, in particular, disbursed about 500,000 Pounds, and the reimbursements, in the whole, did not exceed 60,000 Pounds.

[29] Q. You have said that you pay heavy taxes in Pennsylvania; what do they amount to in the Pound [i.e. in English currency]?

A. The tax on all estates, real and personal, is Eighteen Pence in the Pound, fully rated; and the tax on the profits of trades and professions, with other taxes, do, I suppose, make full Half a Crown in the Pound.

[30] Q. Do you know any thing of the rate of exchange in Pennsylvania, and whether it has fallen lately?

A. It is commonly from 170 to 175. I have heard that it has fallen lately from 175 to 162 and a half, owing, I suppose, to their lessening their orders for goods; and when their debts to this country are paid, I think the exchange will probably be at par.

[31] Q. Do not you think the people of America would submit to pay the stamp duty, if it was moderated?

A. No, never, unless compelled by force of arms.

[32] Q. Are not the taxes in Pennsylvania laid on unequally, in order to burthen the English trade, particularly the tax on professions and business?

A. It is not more burthensome in proportion than the tax on lands. It is intended, and supposed to take an equal proportion of profits.

[33] Q. How is the assembly composed? Of what kinds of people are the members, landholders or traders?

A. It is composed of landholders, merchants and artificers.

[34] Q. Are not the majority landholders?

A. I believe they are.

[35] Q. Do not they, as much as possible, shift the tax off from the land, to ease that, and lay the burthen heavier on trade?

A. I have never understood it so. I never heard such a thing suggested. And indeed an attempt of that kind could answer no purpose. The merchant or trader is always skilled in figures, and ready with his pen and ink. If unequal burthens are laid on his trade, he puts an additional price on his goods; and the consumers, who are chiefly landholders, finally pay the greatest part, if not the whole."

Grey Cooper was a secretary to the Treasury Minister and member of Parliament; there was no rule against multiple office holding and no provision for separation of power in the English government (as was true of Conway, serving in both ministerial and legislative capacities). Cooper had been a member of the Country faction, those not closely aligned with the Crown, in Britain for many years, and was accounted a friend of the colonies. His questions came after Grenville's second round and showed the deference to Franklin expected of someone in Rockingham's administration.

"[36] Q. What was the temper of America towards Great-Britain before the year 1763?

A. The best in the world. They submitted willingly to the government of the Crown, and paid, in all their courts, obedience to acts of parliament. Numerous as the people are in the several old provinces, they cost you nothing in forts, citadels, garrisons or armies, to keep them in subjection. They were governed by this country at the expence only of a little pen, ink and paper. They were led by a thread. They had not only a respect, but an affection, for Great-Britain, for its laws, its customs and manners, and even a fondness for its fashions, that greatly increased the commerce. Natives of Britain were always treated with particular regard; to be an Old England-man was, of itself, a character of some respect, and gave a kind of rank among us.

[37] Q. And what is their temper now?

A. O, very much altered.

[38] Q. Did you ever hear the authority of parliament to make laws for America questioned till lately?

A. The authority of parliament was allowed to be valid in all laws, except such as should lay internal taxes. It was never disputed in laying duties to regulate commerce."

Again Grey Cooper to the rescue.

"[39] Q. In what proportion hath population increased in America?

A. I think the inhabitants of all the provinces together, taken at a medium, double in about 25 years. But their demand for British manufactures increases much faster, as the consumption is not merely in proportion to their numbers, but grows with the growing abilities of the same numbers to pay for them. In 1723, the whole importation from Britain to Pennsylvania, was but about 15,000 Pounds Sterling; it is now near Half a Million."

This calculation of population increase, like many of the other figures that Franklin gave out so precisely and confidently, was partly his own invention. There were colonial census and tax figures, some of which he published, but these were no more precise than his own statistics. At best they were approximations; at worst they were simply fabrications. The more important point is that he was asked for precise figures and gave them—a proof of the growing importance of demographic and economic data in the framing of policy in the home country and the colonies.[48]

"[40] Q. In what light did the people of America use[d] to consider the parliament of Great-Britain?

A. They considered the parliament as the great bulwark and security of their liberties and privileges, and always spoke of it with the utmost respect and veneration. Arbitrary ministers, they thought, might possibly, at times, attempt to oppress them; but they relied on it, that the parliament, on application, would always give redress. They remembered, with gratitude, a strong instance of this, when a bill was brought into parliament, with a clause to make royal instructions laws in the Colonies, which the house of commons would not pass, and it was thrown out.

[41] Q. And have they not still the same respect for parliament?

A. No; it is greatly lessened.

[42] Q. To what causes is that owing?

A. To a concurrence of causes; the restraints lately laid on their trade, by which the bringing of foreign gold and silver into the Colonies was prevented; the prohibition of making paper money among themselves;

and then demanding a new and heavy tax by stamps; taking away, at the same time, trials by juries, and refusing to receive and hear their humble petitions."

Another Grenville query, followed by a somewhat emboldened Franklin response:

"[43] Q. Don't you think they would submit to the stamp-act, if it was modified, the obnoxious parts taken out, and the duty reduced to some particulars, of small moment?

A. No; they will never submit to it."

Rockingham again, perhaps worried by the tone that Franklin had taken. The questions gave Franklin the chance to approach the subject of a tax from a different perspective.

"[44] Q. What do you think is the reason that the people of America increase faster than in England?

A. Because they marry younger, and more generally.

[45] Q. Why so?

A. Because any young couple that are industrious, may easily obtain land of their own, on which they can raise a family.

[46] Q. Are not the lower rank of people more at their ease in America than in England?

A. They may be so, if they are sober and diligent, as they are better paid for their labour.

[47] Q. What is your opinion of a future tax, imposed on the same principle with that of the stamp-act; how would the Americans receive it?

A. Just as they do this. They would not pay it."

But Grenville was neither fooled by Rockingham's tone nor mollified by Franklin's answers. Perhaps a different approach to the same subject—American illegal resistance to a lawful act of Parliament—would trap Franklin? Franklin's response was one that he had worked out over the course of many years: Let the colonists tax themselves and supply Britain with a voluntary contribution. He had broached the idea at the Albany conference of 1754 and gotten the delegates to accede to it, but it was rejected by every colonial legislature to which it was proposed. Thus Franklin could offer no concrete evidence that the colonial legislatures would accept a requisition plan.[49]

"[48] Q. Have you not heard of the resolutions of this house, and of the house of lords, asserting the right of parliament relating to America, including a power to tax the people there?

A. Yes, I have heard of such resolutions.

[49] Q. What will be the opinion of the Americans on those resolutions?

A. They will think them unconstitutional, and unjust.

[50] Q. Was it an opinion in America before 1763, that the parliament had no right to lay taxes and duties there?

A. I never heard any objection to the right of laying duties to regulate commerce; but a right to lay internal taxes was never supposed to be in parliament, as we are not represented there.

[51] Q. On what do you found your opinion, that the people in America made any such distinction?

A. I know that whenever the subject has occurred in conversation where I have been present, it has appeared to be the opinion of every one, that we could not be taxed in a parliament where we were not represented. But the payment of duties laid by act of parliament, as regulations of commerce, was never disputed.

[52] Q. But can you name any act of assembly, or public act of any of your governments, that made such distinction?

A. I do not know that there was any; I think there was never an occasion to make any such act, till now that you have attempted to tax us;

that has occasioned resolutions of assembly, declaring the distinction, in which I think every assembly on the continent, and every member in every assembly, have been unanimous.

[53] Q. What then could occasion conversations on that subject before that time?

A. There was in 1754 a proposition made (I think it came from hence) that in case of a war, which was then apprehended, the governors of the Colonies should meet, and order the levying of troops, building of forts, and taking every other necessary measure for the general defence; and should draw on the treasury here for the sums expended, which were afterwards to be raised in the Colonies by a general tax, to be laid on them by act of parliament. This occasioned a good deal of conversation on the subject, and the general opinion was, that the parliament neither would nor could lay any tax on us, till we were duly represented in parliament, because it was not just, nor agreeable to the nature of an English constitution."

But Grenville had a precedent in mind that ran in the opposite direction. This was not a question at all, but an attempt to refute Franklin's hemming and hawing.

"[54] Q. Don't you know there was a time in New-York, when it was under consideration to make an application to parliament to lay taxes on that Colony, upon a deficiency arising from the assembly's refusing or neglecting to raise the necessary supplies for the support of the civil government?

A. I never heard of it."

Not only had Franklin "heard of it," he proposed such a direct tax on alcoholic spirits. (Franklin did not drink alcohol.) Whether Grenville knew this or not, he did not use that fact to impeach Franklin's examination, but Franklin must have been squirming at the prospect.

"[55] Q. There was such an application under consideration in New-York; and do you apprehend they could suppose the right of parliament to lay a tax in America was only local, and confined to the case of a deficiency in a particular Colony, by a refusal of its assembly to raise the necessary supplies?

> A. They could not suppose such a case, as that the assembly would not raise the necessary supplies to support its own government. An assembly that would refuse it must want common sense, which cannot be supposed. I think there was never any such case at New-York, and that it must be a misrepresentation, or the fact must be misunderstood. I know there have been some attempts, by ministerial instructions from hence, to oblige the assemblies to settle permanent salaries on governors, which they wisely refused to do; but I believe no assembly of New-York, or any other Colony, ever refused duly to support government by proper allowances, from time to time, to public officers.

[56] Q. But in case a governor, acting by instruction, should call on an assembly to raise the necessary supplies, and the assembly should refuse to do it, do you not think it would then be for the good of the people of the colony, as well as necessary to government, that the parliament should tax them?

> A. I do not think it would be necessary. If an assembly could possibly be so absurd as to refuse raising the supplies requisite for the maintenance of government among them, they could not long remain in such a situation; the disorders and confusion occasioned by it must soon bring them to reason.

[57] Q. If it should not, ought not the right to be in Great-Britain of applying a remedy?

> A. A right only to be used in such a case, I should have no objection to, supposing it to be used merely for the good of the people of the Colony.

[58] Q. But who is to judge of that, Britain or the Colony?

> A. Those that feel can best judge."

Grenville's recitation of facts and Franklin's sudden amnesia had him on the ropes, but Grenville needed a knockout punch. Instead of turning to the fact that the colonists had illegally and violently disobeyed Parliament, he allowed Franklin to discuss the difference between internal or direct taxation (a stamp tax for example) and external taxation (the imposition of customs duties or other fees under the Navigation Acts).

The Navigation Acts, dating back to 1651 and by 1765 numbering in the three figures, regulated colonial trade, keeping it within the empire, in British or colonial registered ships, and requiring that certain "enumerated" goods like tobacco go first to British ports. The digression let Franklin catch his breath and descended into a discourse on the quality of colonial woolens (which by an act of Parliament in 1699 were not to be imported into England), mutton, and other equally illuminating subjects.[50]

"[59] Q. You say the Colonies have always submitted to external taxes, and object to the right of parliament only in laying internal taxes; now can you shew that there is any kind of difference between the two taxes to the Colony on which they may be laid?

A. I think the difference is very great. An external tax is a duty laid on commodities imported; that duty is added to the first cost, and other charges on the commodity, and when it is offered to sale, makes a part of the price. If the people do not like it at that price, they refuse it; they are not obliged to pay it. But an internal tax is forced from the people without their consent, if not laid by their own representatives. The stamp-act says, we shall have no commerce, make no exchange of property with each other, neither purchase nor grant, nor recover debts; we shall neither marry, nor make our wills, unless we pay such and such sums, and thus it is intended to extort our money from us, or ruin us by the consequences of refusing to pay it.

[60] Q. But supposing the external tax or duty to be laid on the necessaries of life imported into your Colony, will not that be the same thing in its effects as an internal tax?

A. I do not know a single article imported into the Northern Colonies, but what they can either do without, or make themselves.

[61] Q. Don't you think cloth from England absolutely necessary to them?

A. No, by no means absolutely necessary; with industry and good management, they may very well supply themselves with all they want.

[62] Q. Will it not take a long time to establish that manufacture among them? and must they not in the mean while suffer greatly?

A. I think not. They have made a surprising progress already. And I am of opinion, that before their old clothes are worn out, they will have new ones of their own making.

[63] Q. Can they possibly find wool enough in North-America?

A. They have taken steps to increase the wool. They entered into general combinations to eat no more lamb, and very few lambs were killed last year. This course persisted in, will soon make a prodigious difference in the quantity of wool. And the establishing of great manufactories, like those in the clothing towns here, is not necessary, as it is where the business is to be carried on for the purposes of trade. The people will all spin, and work for themselves, in their own houses.

[64] Q. Can there be wool and manufacture enough in one or two years?

A. In three years, I think, there may.

[65] Q. Does not the severity of the winter, in the Northern Colonies, occasion the wool to be of bad quality?

A. No; the wool is very fine and good.

[66] Q. In the more Southern Colonies, as in Virginia; don't you know that the wool is coarse, and only a kind of hair?

A. I don't know it. I never heard it. Yet I have been sometimes in Virginia. I cannot say I ever took particular notice of the wool there, but I believe it is good, though I cannot speak positively of it; but Virginia, and the Colonies south of it, have less occasion for wool; their winters are short, and not very severe, and they can very well clothe themselves with linen and cotton of their own raising for the rest of the year.

[67] Q. Are not the people, in the more Northern Colonies, obliged to fodder their sheep all the winter?

A. In some of the most Northern Colonies they may be obliged to do it some part of the winter."

It is hard not to imagine a murmur of ribald guffaws and snickering about the foddering of sheep rising from the members as Rockingham regained the floor to ask a more pointed question: whether the colonists would be content with a declaration of right to legislate, a proposal already in the works. In fact, it would not contain an explicit statement on the right to impose taxes, and Franklin would be content with it.[51]

"[68] Q. Considering the resolutions of parliament, as to the right, do you think, if the stamp-act is repealed, that the North Americans will be satisfied?

A. I believe they will.

[69] Q. Why do you think so?

A. I think the resolutions of right will give them very little concern, if they are never attempted to be carried into practice. The Colonies will probably consider themselves in the same situation, in that respect, with Ireland; they know you claim the same right with regard to Ireland, but you never exercise it. And they may believe you never will exercise it in the Colonies, any more than in Ireland, unless on some very extraordinary occasion."

Grenville would not be put off, however, not by the humor his most recent questions had occasioned (he was reputed to have little sense of humor himself) nor by Rockingham's intervention. He had, at any rate, recovered from the woolens digression and sought once again to discomfit Franklin with facts about colonial reluctance to finance war. This time Franklin either had the facts at his command or decided to punch back with his own facts.

"[70] Q. But who are to be the judges of that extraordinary occasion? Is it not the parliament?

A. Though the parliament may judge of the occasion, the people will think it can never exercise such right, till representatives from the Colonies are admitted into parliament, and that whenever the occasion arises, representatives will be ordered.

[71] Q. Did you never hear that Maryland, during the last war, had refused to furnish a quota towards the common defence?

A. Maryland has been much misrepresented in that matter. Maryland, to my knowledge, never refused to contribute, or grant aids to the Crown. The assemblies every year, during the war, voted considerable sums, and formed bills to raise them. The bills were, according to the constitution of that province, sent up to the council, or upper house, for concurrence, that they might be presented to the governor, in order to be enacted into laws. Unhappy disputes between the two houses arising, from the defects of that constitution principally, rendered all the bills but one or two abortive. The proprietary's council rejected them. It is true Maryland did not contribute its proportion, but it was, in my opinion, the fault of the government, not of the people.

[72] Q. Was it not talked of in the other provinces as a proper measure to apply to parliament to compel them?

A. I have heard such discourse; but as it was well known, that the people were not to blame, no such application was ever made, nor any step taken towards it.

[73] Q. Was it not proposed at a public meeting?

A. Not that I know of."

Franklin was in England during the colonial protests, but surely the newspapers brought him the information to which Grenville referred. Franklin also knew that the linchpin of colonial administration was the royal governor or, if he elected to remain in Britain, the lieutenant governor in the colony. In fact, during his stay in England, Franklin was angling to become the royal governor of Pennsylvania, should the crown decide to end proprietary rule there. Some of the royal governors, notably William Cosby in New York, were so rapacious and so hated that the system nearly collapsed until the governor was recalled and replaced. Conway's mentor and predecessor, the Duke of Newcastle, was responsible for some of these flaps (he selected Cosby, for example), and Conway may have been worried that a similar situation was developing in Massachusetts with Lieutenant Governor Thomas Hutchinson's role in the Stamp Act crisis—hence the next set of questions, about paper currency in Massachusetts.[52]

"[74] Q. Do you remember the abolishing of the paper currency in New England, by act of assembly?

A. I do remember its being abolished, in the Massachusetts Bay.

[75] Q. Was not Lieutenant Governor Hutchinson principally concerned in that transaction?

A. I have heard so.

[76] Q. Was it not at that time a very unpopular law?

A. I believe it might, though I can say little about it, as I lived at a distance from that province.

[77] Q. Was not the scarcity of gold and silver an argument used against abolishing the paper?

A. I suppose it was.

[78] Q. What is the present opinion there of that law? Is it as unpopular as it was at first?

A. I think it is not.

[79] Q. Have not instructions from hence been sometimes sent over to governors, highly oppressive and unpolitical?

A. Yes.

[80] Q. Have not some governors dispensed with them for that reason?

A. Yes, I have heard so."

Grenville again, this time pressing at the other end of Franklin's argument. If the stamp tax was not acceptable, was the Sugar Act not acquiesced in? Grenville had sent ships to patrol the coast of North America to ensure obedience to the Sugar Act. What would it take for an internal tax act to be enforced?

"[81] Q. Did the Americans ever dispute the controlling power of parliament to regulate the commerce?

A. No.

[82] Q. Can any thing less than a military force carry the stamp-act into execution?

A. I do not see how a military force can be applied to that purpose.

[83] Q. Why may it not?

A. Suppose a military force sent into America, they will find nobody in arms; what are they then to do? They cannot force a man to take stamps who chooses to do without them. They will not find a rebellion; they may indeed make one."

Franklin was not entirely candid here. There were muskets, fowling pieces, and all manner of other firearms in the colonies. Just how many remains controversial, but whether more than half of the households had serviceable firearms (the best estimate) or not, Franklin knew perfectly well about the colonists' possession of firearms from the "Paxton Boys" raids on peaceful Indian settlements at the end of the French and Indian War. During that war, he had toured the frontier of Pennsylvania as part of a diplomatic mission to the Indians. He would then have seen a good many firearms.[53]

"[84] Q. If the act is not repealed, what do you think will be the consequences?

A. A total loss of the respect and affection the people of America bear to this country, and of all the commerce that depends on that respect and affection.

[85] Q. How can the commerce be affected?

A. You will find, that if the act is not repealed, they will take very little of your manufactures in a short time.

[86] Q. Is it in their power to do without them?

A. I think they may very well do without them.

[87] Q. Is it their interest not to take them?

A. The goods they take from Britain are either necessaries, mere conveniences, or superfluities. The first, as cloth, &c. with a little industry they can make at home; the second they can do without, till they are able to provide them among themselves; and the last, which are much the greatest part, they will strike off immediately. They are mere articles of fashion, purchased and consumed, because the fashion in a respected country, but will now be detested and rejected. The people have already struck off, by general agreement, the use of all goods fashionable in mournings, and many thousand pounds worth are sent back as unsaleable."

Franklin was again either prescient or he had heard whispers of a plan for nonimportation or even nonconsumption of British trade goods. When, after the Declaratory Act passed, Parliament followed the suggestion of incoming

Chancellor of the Exchequer Charles Townshend to impose new customs duties on tea, paper, paint, lead, and the like, Boston proposed a general nonimportation policy on British goods. In the end, British merchants convinced Parliament to repeal all of the new duties save that on tea. The movement to shift from imported cloth to homespun, while much celebrated among the patriots, did not much dent colonial buyers' desire for imported fabrics.[54]

"[88] Q. Is it their interest to make cloth at home?

A. I think they may at present get it cheaper from Britain, I mean of the same fineness and neatness of workmanship; but when one considers other circumstances, the restraints on their trade, and the difficulty of making remittances, it is their interest to make every thing.

[89] Q. Suppose an act of internal regulations, connected with a tax, how would they receive it?

A. I think it would be objected to.

[90] Q. Then no regulation with a tax would be submitted to?

A. Their opinion is, that when aids to the Crown are wanted, they are to be asked of the several assemblies, according to the old established usage, who will, as they always have done, grant them freely. And that their money ought not to be given away without their consent, by persons at a distance, unacquainted with their circumstances and abilities. The granting aids to the Crown, is the only means they have of recommending themselves to their sovereign, and they think it extremely hard and unjust, that a body of men, in which they have no representatives, should make a merit to itself of giving and granting what is not its own, but theirs, and deprive them of a right they esteem of the utmost value and importance, as it is the security of all their other rights."

Grenville knew that as colonial postmaster Franklin was getting paid. Patronage was the grease that made the imperial machine run smoothly. The alternative, royal salaries for all officers, would undermine the very purpose of the empire: a favorable balance of trade for the home country. By pressing Franklin on the cost a royal post office imposed on the colonists, Grenville was making the issue personal. But he could also ply the logic of such costs to include all colonial imports and exports. Franklin was up to the task: He made

a distinction between impositions that paid for services and impositions meant to raise a revenue for other purposes. The problem with his answer was that the Stamp Act revenue was to pay for troops quartered in the colonies. Were these a service to the colonists or a police force imposed on them?

"[91] Q. But is not the post-office, which they have long received, a tax as well as a regulation?

A. No; the money paid for the postage of a letter is not of the nature of a tax; it is merely a quantum meruit [literally "what is owed"] for a service done; no person is compellable to pay the money, if he does not chuse to receive the service. A man may still, as before the act, send his letter by a servant, a special messenger, or a friend, if he thinks it cheaper and safer.

[92] Q. But do they not consider the regulations of the post-office, by the act of last year, as a tax?

A. By the regulations of last year the rate of postage was generally abated near thirty per cent. through all America; they certainly cannot consider such abatement as a tax.

[93] Q. If an excise was laid by a parliament, which they might likewise avoid paying, by not consuming the articles excised, would they then not object to it?

A. They would certainly object to it, as an excise is unconnected with any service done, and is merely an aid which they think ought to be asked of them, and granted by them, if they are to pay it, and can be granted for them by no others whatsoever, whom they have not impowered for the purpose.

[94] Q. You say they do not object to the right of parliament in laying duties on goods to be paid on their importation; now, is there any kind of difference between a duty on the importation of goods, and an excise on their consumption?

A. Yes; a very material one; an excise, for the reasons I have just mentioned, they think you can have no right to lay within their country. But the sea is yours; you maintain, by your fleets, the safety of navigation in it; and keep it clear of pirates; you may have therefore a natural and equitable right to some toll or duty on merchandizes carried through that part of your dominions, towards defraying the expence you are at in ships to maintain the safety of that carriage.

[95] Q. Does this reasoning hold in the case of a duty laid on the produce of their lands exported? And would they not then object to such a duty?

A. If it tended to make the produce so much dearer abroad as to lessen the demand for it, to be sure they would object to such a duty; not to your right of laying it, but they would complain of it as a burthen, and petition you to lighten it.

[96] Q. Is not the duty paid on the tobacco exported a duty of that kind?

A. That, I think, is only on tobacco carried coastwise from one Colony to another, and appropriated as a fund for supporting the college at Williamsburg, in Virginia."

Grenville tried another tack, this one taking him into West Indian waters. The British colonies in the Caribbean were far too dependent on the goodwill of the home country, and the protection of the royal navy, to join in the Stamp Act revolt as fully as the mainland colonies. The legislatures of Jamaica and Barbados protested, to be sure, but the handful of white settlers, surrounded by a sea of black slaves, could hardly raise disorder without endangering their own lives and fortunes.[55]

"[97] Q. Have not the assemblies in the West-Indies the same natural rights with those in North America?

A. Undoubtedly.

[98] Q. And is there not a tax laid there on their sugars exported?

A. I am not much acquainted with the West-Indies, but the duty of four and a half per cent. on sugars exported, was, I believe, granted by their own assemblies."

Point to Grenville. But again he seemed to wander in following it up. A question on poll taxes seemed to have no mooring, and Franklin easily replied to it. Poll or head taxes on "bachelors" (the statute actually was the first time that the term was used for unmarried men) was actually a tax reform in which adult men who had no family to support or who lived with their family anted up something for the public treasury to fund poorhouses and other social

services. The Pennsylvania bachelor tax lasted from the founding of the colony to 1780. Grenville was fishing here, however, looking for some colonial version of an internal tax comparable to the stamp tax.[56]

The next set questions gave Franklin the chance to explore the nonimportation theme, recognizing that the manufacturers whose goods the British merchants sold in the colonies, and the exporters of foreign goods to the colonies, had many friends in Parliament.[57]

"[99] Q. How much is the poll-tax in your province laid on unmarried men?

A. It is, I think, Fifteen Shillings, to be paid by every single freeman, upwards of twenty-one years old.

[100] Q. What is the annual amount of all the taxes in Pennsylvania?

A. I suppose about 20,000 Pounds sterling.

[101] Q. Supposing the stamp-act continued, and enforced, do you imagine that ill humour will induce the Americans to give as much for worse manufactures of their own, and use them, preferably to better of ours?

A. Yes, I think so. People will pay as freely to gratify one passion as another, their resentment as their pride.

[102] Q. Would the people at Boston discontinue their trade?

A. The merchants are a very small number, compared with the body of the people, and must discontinue their trade, if nobody will buy their goods.

[103] Q. What are the body of the people in the Colonies?

A. They are farmers, husbandmen or planters.

[104] Q. Would they suffer the produce of their lands to rot?

A. No; but they would not raise so much. They would manufacture more, and plough less."

Getting nowhere slowly, Grenville tried yet another tack: If stamps were necessary for all civil business, how could the local governments function without them? He wanted to push Franklin into a corner where the only

answer was a defense of the antistamp riots. Most of the members would have known that Franklin had not opposed the Act very vigorously and had proposed his friend John Hughes as Pennsylvania stamp distributor. Thus Grenville's questions were Archbishop Morton's fork: Either Franklin must admit that the colonists were lawless and condemn them or defend the colonists and admit that he was himself opposed to parliamentary authority. But Franklin had a ready answer: The distributors had quit.[58]

"[105] Q. Would they live without the administration of justice in civil matters, and suffer all the inconveniences of such a situation for any considerable time, rather than to take the stamps, supposing the stamps were protected by a sufficient force, where every one might have them?

A. I think the supposition impracticable, that the stamps should be so protected as that every one might have them. The act requires sub-distributors to be appointed in every county town, district and village, and they would be necessary. But the principal distributors, who were to have had a considerable profit on the whole, have not thought it worth while to continue in the office, and I think it impossible to find sub-distributors fit to be trusted, who, for the trifling profit that must come to their share, would incur the odium, and run the hazard that would attend it; and if they could be found, I think it impracticable to protect the stamps in so many distant and remote places.

[106] Q. But in places where they could be protected, would not the people use them rather than remain in such a situation, unable to obtain any right, or recover, by law, any debt?

A. It is hard to say what they would do. I can only judge what other people will think, and how they will act, by what I feel within myself. I have a great many debts due to me in America, and I had rather they should remain unrecoverable by any law, than submit to the stamp-act. They will be debts of honour. It is my opinion the people will either continue in that situation, or find some way to extricate themselves, perhaps by generally agreeing to proceed in the courts without stamps.

[107] Q. What do you think a sufficient military force to protect the distribution of the stamps in every part of America?

A. A very great force; I can't say what, if the disposition of America is for a general resistance.

[108] Q. What is the number of men in America able to bear arms, or of disciplined militia?

A. There are, I suppose, at least—[Question objected to. He withdrew. Called in again.]"

Someone had interrupted Grenville, perhaps an ally, for Grenville had verged on saying what, to this time, was unspeakable—a standing army in time of peace to enforce the law. In fact, Hutchinson and his superiors were already considering the dispatch of regular troops to Boston to prevent rioting like that of the summer of 1765.[59]

"[109] Q. Is the American stamp-act an equal tax on that country?

A. I think not.

[110] Q. Why so?

A. The greatest part of the money must arise from law suits for the recovery of debts, and be paid by the lower sort of people, who were too poor easily to pay their debts. It is therefore a heavy tax on the poor, and a tax upon them for being poor.

[111] Q. But will not this increase of expence be a means of lessening the number of law suits?

A. I think not; for as the costs all fall upon the debtor, and are to be paid by him, they would be no discouragement to the creditor to bring his action.

[112] Q. Would it not have the effect of excessive usury?

A. Yes, as an oppression of the debtor."

Conway once more interjected questions designed less to accuse or blame than to gain information about the colonies Conway's interest in Ireland was natural, as he had been Chief Secretary for Ireland for two years, from 1755 to 1757. His duties in that office included supervision of the Irish House of Commons.

"[113] Q. How many ships are there laden annually in North-America with flax-seed for Ireland?

A. I cannot speak to the number of ships, but I know that in 1752, 10,000 hogsheads of flax-seed, each containing 7 bushels, were exported from Philadelphia to Ireland. I suppose the quantity is greatly increased since that time; and it is understood that the exportation from New York is equal to that from Philadelphia.

[114] Q. What becomes of the flax that grows with that flax-seed?

A. They manufacture some into coarse, and some into a middling kind of linen.

[115] Q. Are there any slitting mills [a mill used in the process of making iron nails] in America?

A. I think there are, but I believe only one at present employed. I suppose they will all be set to work, if the interruption of the trade continues.

[116] Q. Are there any fulling mills [a mill used in clothmaking] there?

A. A great many.

[117] Q. Did you never hear that a great quantity of stockings were contracted for the army, during the war, and manufactured in Philadelphia?

A. I have heard so."

Listening to Conway and Franklin discuss linens and nails, Grenville must have grown frustrated. He had not spent the better part of his life as a lawyer in government service to now give up a case without a final effort to win it. Of course, it was already lost, and he knew it, but habits of a lifetime die hard. He realized that a repeal act was coming, followed by a declaratory act, and he wanted Franklin to admit that the retreat of Parliament would only encourage more dissent in the colonies.

"[118] Q. If the stamp act should be repealed, would not the Americans think they could oblige the parliament to repeal every external tax law now in force?

A. It is hard to answer questions of what people at such a distance will think.

[119] Q. But what do you imagine they will think were the motives of repealing the act?

> A. I suppose they will think that it was repealed from a conviction of its inexpediency; and they will rely upon it, that while the same inexpediency subsists, you will never attempt to make such another.

[120] Q. What do you mean by its inexpediency?

> A. I mean its inexpediency on several accounts; the poverty and inability of those who were to pay the tax; the general discontent it has occasioned; and the impracticability of enforcing it.

[121] Q. If the act should be repealed, and the legislature should shew its resentment to the opposers of the stamp-act, would the Colonies acquiesce in the authority of the legislature? What is your opinion they would do?

> A. I don't doubt at all, that if the legislature repeal the stamp-act, the Colonies will acquiesce in the authority."

One would like to think the next set of questions came from Rockingham supporter Edmund Burke (Rockingham's private secretary). Burke's place in Parliament and the patronage he enjoyed came in large measure from his association with Rockingham, but Burke was also a political thinker on his own. Though he had only won his seat in December 1765, he spoke eloquently against the Stamp Act in his maiden speech, on January 27, 1766, presenting a petition from his constituents in Manchester against the Act, and later, more fulsomely, on February 3, in favor of the Declaratory Act. He would support the American cause during the crisis of the 1770s and throughout the war for independence.[60]

Because Burke's two addresses eloquently balanced the case for colonial representation and the absolute authority of Parliament in making policy for the colonies, and because the applause he gained for his eloquence in Parliament might have afforded him license to question Franklin on these same issues, it seems plausible to name him as Franklin's interrogator here. In fact, we do not know from internal evidence who asked the next set of questions, but they laid the foundation for Franklin's most thoughtful contribution to the debate, an excursus into practical political theory. He could not argue for self-government much less for the sovereignty of the colonies (though only a sovereign state can claim to lay taxes), but he could make the case for a limited form of colonial autonomy. He laid that claim on the basis of fact—that the colonies were in many ways domestically autonomous already. It would have been but a small step further for Franklin to conclude, as Thomas

Jefferson and the other revolutionaries did in 1774 and 1775, that the colonies should be ruled by the people of the colonies because it was these people, and not the British government, who made the colonies prosperous. Franklin had thus to walk a fine line between submission to parliamentary authority (at least in principle) and colonial independence. That he did just that with aplomb was a tribute to his savvy as much as to his experience with government in Pennsylvania. No answer before or after was as long as this, a practical and frank mini-essay on the governance of the colonies.

Such essays were already flowing back and forth across the Atlantic. The most influential of these, former Massachusetts Governor Thomas Pownall's The Administration of the Colonies *(1764), started life as a pamphlet and ended up a book. Pownall was not the clearest thinker, but his central argument was similar in some ways to Franklin's: efficiency with an eye to the mutual interests of crown and colonies. Franklin's own essays and his proposals for the Plan of Union at Albany can all be found in microcosm in this little speech.*[61]

"[122] Q. But if the legislature should think fit to ascertain its right to lay taxes, by any act laying a small tax, contrary to their opinion, would they submit to pay the tax?

A. The proceedings of the people in America have been considered too much together. The proceedings of the assemblies have been very different from those of the mobs, and should be distinguished, as having no connection with each other. The assemblies have only peaceably resolved what they take to be their rights; they have taken no measures for opposition by force; they have not built a fort, raised a man, or provided a grain of ammunition, in order to such opposition. The ringleaders of riots they think ought to be punished; they would punish them themselves, if they could. Every sober sensible man would wish to see rioters punished; as otherwise peaceable people have no security of person or estate. But as to any internal tax, how small soever, laid by the legislature here on the people there, while they have no representatives in this legislature, I think it will never be submitted to. They will oppose it to the last. They do not consider it as at all necessary for you to raise money on them by your taxes, because they are, and always have been, ready to raise money by taxes among themselves, and to grant large sums, equal to their abilities, upon requisition from the Crown. They have not only granted equal to their abilities, but, during all the last war, they granted far beyond their abilities, and beyond their proportion with this country, you yourselves being judges, to the amount of many hundred thousand pounds, and this they did freely and readily, only on a sort of promise from the secretary of state, that it should be recommended to parliament to make them compensation. It was accordingly recommended to parliament, in the most honourable manner, for them. America has been greatly misrepresented and abused here, in papers, and pamphlets, and speeches, as ungrateful, and unreasonable, and unjust, in having put this nation to immense expence for their defence, and refusing to bear any part of that expence. The Colonies raised, paid and clothed, near 25000 men during the last war, a number equal to those sent from Britain, and far beyond their proportion; they went deeply into debt in doing this, and all their taxes and estates are mortgaged, for many years to come, for discharging that debt. Government here was at that time very sensible of this. The Colonies were recommended to parliament. Every year the King sent down to the house a written message to this purpose, That his Majesty, being highly sensible of the zeal and vigour with which his faithful subjects in North-America had exerted themselves, in defence of his Majesty's just rights and possessions, recommended it to the house to take the same into consideration, and enable him to give them a proper compensation. You will find those messages on your own journals every year of the war to the very last, and you did accordingly give 200,000 Pounds annually to the Crown, to be distributed in such compensation to the Colonies. This is the strongest of all proofs that the Colonies, far from being unwilling to bear a share of the burthen, did exceed their proportion; for if they had done less, or had only equalled their proportion, there would have been no room or reason for compensation. Indeed the sums reimbursed them, were by no means adequate to the expence they incurred beyond their proportion; but they never murmured at that; they esteemed their Sovereign's approbation of their zeal and fidelity, and the approbation of this house, far beyond any other kind of compensation; therefore there was no occasion for this act, to force money from a willing people; they had not refused giving money for the purposes of the act; no requisition had been made; they were always willing and ready to do what could reasonably be expected from them, and in this light they wish to be considered."

Although he spoke often and warmly of the people, Franklin was not a radical politician by any means. The "mob" was as much the enemy of liberty, in his thinking, as the tyrant. The mob would never come to the aid of Britain,

but the people of the colonies had and would continued to provide manpower for defense of the empire.[62]

"[123] Q. But suppose Great-Britain should be engaged in a war in Europe, would North-America contribute to the support of it?

A. I do think they would, as far as their circumstances would permit. They consider themselves as a part of the British empire, and as having one common interest with it; they may be looked on here as foreigners, but they do not consider themselves as such. They are zealous for the honour and prosperity of this nation, and, while they are well used, will always be ready to support it, as far as their little power goes. In 1739 they were called upon to assist in the expedition against Carthagena, and they sent 3000 men to join your army. It is true Carthagena is in America, but as remote from the Northern Colonies, as if it had been in Europe. They make no distinction of wars, as to their duty of assisting in them. I know the last war [i.e., the French and Indian War] is commonly spoke of here as entered into for the defence, or for the sake of the people of America. I think it is quite misunderstood. It began about the limits between Canada and Nova-Scotia, about territories to which the Crown indeed laid claim, but were not claimed by any British Colony; none of the lands had been granted to any Colonist; we had therefore no particular concern or interest in that dispute. As to the Ohio [River Valley country], the contest there began about your right of trading in the Indian country, a right you had by the treaty of Utrecht [signed in 1713, ending the War of the Spanish Succession, in Europe, and Queen Anne's War in the colonies], which the French infringed; they seized the traders and their goods, which were your manufactures; they took a fort which a company of your merchants, and their factors and correspondents, had erected there, to secure that trade. [General Edward] Braddock was sent with an army to re-take that fort [the French outpost of Fort Duquesne at the fork of the Monongahela and Allegheny rivers—today Pittsburgh] (which was looked on here as another incroachment on the King's territory) and to protect your trade. It was not till after his defeat that the Colonies were attacked. They were before in perfect peace with both French and Indians; the troops were not therefore sent for their defence. The trade with the Indians, though carried on in America, is not an American interest. The people of America are chiefly farmers and planters; scarce any thing that they raise or produce is an article of commerce with the Indians. The Indian trade is a British interest; it is carried on with British manufactures, for the profit of British merchants and manufacturers; therefore the war, as it commenced for the defence of territories of the Crown, the property of no American, and for the defence of a trade purely British, was really a British war—and yet the people of America made no scruple of contributing their utmost towards carrying it on, and bringing it to a happy conclusion."

With this somewhat skewed account of war and peace in the colonies (who could believe that the colonists lived in "perfect peace with the French and the Indians" after the atrocities on both sides during nearly one hundred years of frontier warfare, or that the French and Indian War did not serve colonial land speculators' interest in the West), Franklin had arrived at his intended stopping point: a coordinate system of government, of colonies and home country, rather than an empire in which the colonies were entirely subordinate to the metropolitan power. It was a system that recognized that the interests of the crown were not always those of the colonies—indeed, that many colonists (particularly in Pennsylvania) resented European rivalries leading to war in the colonies.

Grenville was either obdurate or unconvinced by the good will Franklin evinced in his essay on colonial self-government, and he returned to a very different vision of the colonial–home country relationship.

"[124] Q. Do you think then that the taking possession of the King's territorial rights, and strengthening the frontiers, is not an American interest?

A. Not particularly, but conjointly a British and an American interest.

[125] Q. You will not deny that the preceding war, the war with Spain, [i.e., the War of Jenkins' Ear, fought over trade in the West Indies, became part of the far more extensive King George's War, from 1739 to 1748] was entered into for the sake of America; was it not occasioned by captures made in the American seas?

A. Yes; captures of ships carrying on the British trade there, with British manufactures.

[126] Q. Was not the late war with the Indians, since the peace with France, a war for America only?

A. Yes; it was more particularly for America than the former, but it was rather a consequence or remains of the former war, the Indians not having been thoroughly pacified, and the Americans bore by much the greatest share of the expence. It was put an end to by the army under General [actually Colonel Henry] Bouquet; there were not above 300 regulars in that army, and above 1000 Pennsylvanians.

[127] Q. Is it not necessary to send troops to America, to defend the Americans against the Indians?

A. No, by no means; it never was necessary. They defended themselves when they were but an handful, and the Indians much more numerous. They continually gained ground, and have driven the Indians over the mountains, without any troops sent to their assistance from this country. And can it be thought necessary now to send troops for their defence from those diminished Indian tribes, when the Colonies are become so populous, and so strong? There is not the least occasion for it; they are very able to defend themselves.

[128] Q. Do you say there were no more than 300 regular troops employed in the late Indian war?

A. Not on the Ohio, or the frontiers of Pennsylvania, which was the chief part of the war that affected the Colonies. There were garrisons at Niagara, Fort Detroit, and those remote posts kept for the sake of your trade; I did not reckon them, but I believe that on the whole the number of Americans, or provincial troops, employed in the war, was greater than that of the regulars. I am not certain, but I think so."

Franklin must have been deeply tired by this time. He had performed brilliantly, bravely and intelligently negotiating all the obstacles that Grenville laid in his path. Friendly questions allowed him some welcomed respite.

"[129] Q. Do you think the assemblies have a right to levy money on the subject there, to grant to the Crown?

A. I certainly think so; they have always done it.

[130] Q. Are they acquainted with the [English 1688] declaration of rights? And do they know that, by that statute, money is not to be raised on the subject but by consent of parliament?

A. They are very well acquainted with it."

The Declaration of Right, part of the so-called Glorious Revolution of 1689 that replaced King James II with his daughter, Mary, and William of Orange, her Dutch husband, was a resolution that Parliament imposed on the incoming monarchs. It included the key idea that all money bills originated in Parliament. The Declaration and the parliamentary act that followed did not mention the colonies, but parliamentary supremacy over the public treasury in England supposedly extended to the colonies through their original "charters." These provided that the colonial governments could not pass an act contrary to the laws of England. Although the Glorious Revolution left Parliament supreme in England, even after the Glorious Revolution, the king regarded the colonies as his personal possessions. Trying to make sense of this somewhat complex and certainly confusing division of power in England, some colonial leaders took the Declaration of Rights in a more general sense—that is, a declaration that all money bills should originate with representative assemblies. Thus Franklin and his parliamentary interrogators might well have had a different idea of what the Declaration of Rights meant. In any case, colonial protestors against the Townshend Duties of 1767 would embrace this latter notion with the rallying cry "no taxation without representation."[63]

"[131] Q. How then can they think they have a right to levy money for the Crown, or for any other than local purposes?

> A. They understand that clause to relate to subjects only within the realm; that no money can be levied on them for the Crown, but by consent of parliament. The Colonies are not supposed to be within the realm; they have assemblies of their own, which are their parliaments, and they are in that respect, in the same situation with Ireland. When money is to be raised for the Crown upon the subject in Ireland, or in the Colonies, the consent is given in the parliament of Ireland, or in the assemblies of the Colonies. They think the parliament of Great-Britain cannot properly give that consent till it has representatives from America; for the petition of right expressly says, it is to be by common consent in parliament, and the people of America have no representatives in parliament, to make a part of that common consent."

Having made his central point, Franklin was willing to concede that on matters of home country governance, in particular the relationship of

Parliament to the crown, he was not able to advance an opinion. Anything that he said would be out of court—that is, out of his realm of expertise. But one notes how deferentially he answered.

"[132] Q. If the stamp-act should be repealed, and an act should pass, ordering the assemblies of the Colonies to indemnify the sufferers by the riots, would they obey it?

A. That is a question I cannot answer.

[133] Q. Suppose the King should require the Colonies to grant a revenue, and the parliament should be against their doing it, do they think they can grant a revenue to the King, without the consent of the parliament of G. Britain?

A. That is a deep question. As to my own opinion, I should think myself at liberty to do it, and should do it, if I liked the occasion.

[134] Q. When money has been raised in the Colonies, upon requisitions, has it not been granted to the King?

A. Yes, always; but the requisitions have generally been for some service expressed, as to raise, clothe and pay troops, and not for money only.

[135] Q. If the act should pass, requiring the American assemblies to make compensation to the sufferers, and they should disobey it, and then the parliament should, by another act, lay an internal tax, would they then obey it?

A. The people will pay no internal tax; and I think an act to oblige the assemblies to make compensation is unnecessary, for I am of opinion, that as soon as the present heats are abated, they will take the matter into consideration, and, if it is right to be done, they will do it of themselves."

Finally, Conway finished the ordeal by asking about the colonial post.

"[136] Q. Do not letters often come into the post-offices in America, directed to some inland town where no post goes?

A. Yes.

[137] Q. Can any private person take up those letters, and carry them as directed?

A. Yes; any friend of the person may do it, paying the postage that has occurred.

[138] Q. But must he not pay an additional postage for the distance to such inland town?

A. No.

[139] Q. Can the post-master answer delivering the letter, without being paid such additional postage?

A. Certainly he can demand nothing, where he does no service.

[140] Q. Suppose a person, being far from home, finds a letter in a post-office directed to him, and he lives in a place to which the post generally goes, and the letter is directed to that place, will the post-master deliver him the letter, without his paying the postage receivable at the place to which the letter is directed?

A. Yes; the office cannot demand postage for a letter that it does not carry, or farther than it does carry it."

But Grenville would not let Franklin go without one last riposte. This time the subject was ferrymen.

"[141] Q. Are not ferryman in America obliged, by act of parliament, to carry over the posts without pay?

A. Yes.

[142] Q. Is not this a tax on the ferryman?

A. They do not consider it as such, as they have an advantage from persons travelling with the post."

Time to close, and Rockingham appointed himself conductor of the coda.

"[143] Q. If the stamp-act should be repealed, and the Crown should make a requisition to the Colonies for a sum of money, would they grant it?

A. I believe they would.

[144] Q. Why do you think so?

A. I can speak for the Colony I live in; I had it in instruction from the assembly to assure the ministry, that as they always had done, so they should always think it their duty to grant such aids to the Crown as were suitable to their circumstances and abilities, whenever called upon for the purpose, in the usual constitutional manner; and I had the honour of communicating this instruction to that honourable gentleman then minister.

[145] Q. Would they do this for a British concern; as suppose a war in some part of Europe, that did not affect them?

A. Yes, for any thing that concerned the general interest. They consider themselves as a part of the whole.

[146] Q. What is the usual constitutional manner of calling on the Colonies for aids?

A. A letter from the secretary of state.

[147] Q. Is this all you mean, a letter from the secretary of state?

A. I mean the usual way of requisition, in a circular letter from the secretary of state, by his Majesty's command, reciting the occasion, and recommending it to the Colonies to grant such aids as became their loyalty, and were suitable to their abilities.

[148] Q. Did the secretary of state ever write for money for the Crown?

A. The requisitions have been to raise, clothe and pay men, which cannot be done without money.

[149] Q. Would they grant money alone, if called on?

A. In my opinion they would, money as well as men, when they have money, or can make it.

[150] Q. If the parliament should repeal the stamp-act, will the assembly of Pennsylvania rescind their resolutions?

A. I think not."

In what appears to be almost an afterthought, but a thought that Franklin knew was in the minds of members of the House of Commons, because he had raised it in other contexts and Grenville had spoken about it when the Act was first debated, came the matter of colonial representation in Parliament. It is unclear if these questions were friendly or not; I rather think they were not.

"[151] Q. Before there was any thought of the stamp-act, did they wish for a representation in parliament?

A. No.

[152] Q. Don't you know that there is, in the Pennsylvania charter, an express reservation of the right of parliament to lay taxes there?

A. I know there is a clause in the charter, by which the King grants that he will levy no taxes on the inhabitants, unless it be with the consent of the assembly, or by act of parliament.

[153] Q. How then could the assembly of Pennsylvania assert, that laying a tax on them by the stamp-act was an infringement of their rights?

A. They understand it thus; by the same charter, and otherwise, they are intitled to all the privileges and liberties of Englishmen; they find in the great charters, and the petition and declaration of rights, that one of the privileges of English subjects is, that they are not to be taxed but by their common consent; they have therefore relied upon it, from the first settlement of the province, that the parliament never would, nor could, by colour of that clause in the charter, assume a right of taxing them, till it had qualified itself to exercise such right, by admitting representatives from the people to be taxed, who ought to make a part of that common consent.

[154] Q. Are there any words in the charter that justify that construction?

A. The common rights of Englishmen, as declared by Magna Charta, and the petition of right, all justify it."

The English Magna Charta or Magna Carta, the great charter of liberties, was exacted from King John at sword-point in 1215. Amended charters

appeared in 1216, 1217, and 1225. They promised much, including a rudimentary guarantee of due process in civil and criminal law, but delivered little, as the barons who demanded these rights soon discovered. Much in it was not realized until the Glorious Revolution, and some parts of it were still not applicable to minorities, women, Catholics, Jews, servants, and foreigners when Franklin cited it. But Grenville may not have meant the Magna Carta; the reference to the "charter" may have been to the charter that King Charles II granted to William Penn, that is, the charter for Pennsylvania. Here confusion could easily occur, for the royal charter for the colony was not the basis for government in it; instead, it William Penn's own Frame of Government *(1682) and its subsequent revisions. These fundamental laws for the colony included far more generous grants of self-government than appeared in the royal charters.*

⁂

"[155] Q. Does the distinction between internal and external taxes exist in the words of the charter?

A. No, I believe not.

[156] Q. Then may they not, by the same interpretation, object to the parliament's right of external taxation?

A. They never have hitherto. Many arguments have been lately used here to shew them that there is no difference, and that if you have no right to tax them internally, you have none to tax them externally, or make any other law to bind them. At present they do not reason so, but in time they may possibly be convinced by these arguments.

[157] Q. Do not the resolutions of the Pennsylvania assembly say all taxes?

A. If they do, they mean only internal taxes; the same words have not always the same meaning here and in the Colonies. By taxes they mean internal taxes; by duties they mean customs; these are their ideas of the language.

[158] Q. Have you not seen the resolutions of the Massachusetts' Bay assembly?

A. I have.

[159] Q. Do they not say, that neither external nor internal taxes can be laid on them by Parliament?

A. I don't know that they do; I believe not.

[160] Q. If the same Colony should say neither tax nor imposition could be laid, does not that province hold the power of parliament can hold neither?

A. I suppose that by the word imposition, they do not intend to express duties to be laid on goods imported, as regulations of commerce.

[161] Q. What can the Colonies mean then by imposition as distinct from taxes?

A. They may mean many things, as impressing of men, or of carriages, quartering troops on private houses, and the like; there may be great impositions, that are not properly taxes."

Clearly Franklin had reached the limit of his ability to inform the members and the limit of his patience, if not his stamina. He was becoming a little testy. The grilling had taken its toll. Grenville hoped, perhaps, that he could outlast Franklin with a last series of questions hinting that Franklin, who gained by his patronage from the postmastership, should have been more conciliatory.

"[162] Q. Is not the post-office rate an internal tax laid by act of parliament?

A. I have answered that.

[163] Q. Are all parts of the Colonies equally able to pay taxes?

A. No, certainly; the frontier parts, which have been ravaged by the enemy, are greatly disabled by that means, and therefore, in such cases, are usually favoured in our tax-laws.

[164] Q. Can we, at this distance, be competent judges of what favours are necessary?

A. The Parliament have supposed it, by claiming a right to make tax laws for America; I think it impossible.

[165] Q. Would the repeal of the stamp-act be any discouragement of your manufactures? Will the people that have begun to manufacture decline it?

A. Yes, I think they will; especially if, at the same time, the trade is opened again, so that remittances can be easily made. I have known several instances that make it probable. In the war before last, tobacco being low, and making little remittance, the people of Virginia went generally into family manufacturers. Afterwards, when tobacco bore a better price, they returned to the use of British manufactures. So fulling mills were very much disused in the last war in Pennsylvania, because bills were then plenty, and remittances could easily be made to Britain for English cloth and other goods.

[166] Q. If the stamp-act should be repealed, would it induce the assemblies of America to acknowledge the rights of parliament to tax them, and would they erase their resolutions?

A. No, never.

[167] Q. Is there no means of obliging them to erase those resolutions?

A. None that I know of; they will never do it unless compelled by force of arms.

[168] Q. Is there a power on earth that can force them to erase them?

A. No power, how great soever, can force men to change their opinions.

[169] Q. Do they consider the post-office as a tax, or as a regulation?

A. Not as a tax, but as a regulation and conveniency; every assembly encouraged it, and supported it in its infancy, by grants of money, which they would not otherwise have done; and the people have always paid the postage.

[170] Q. When did you receive the instructions you mentioned?

A. I brought them with me, when I came to England, about 15 months since.

[171] Q. When did you communicate that instruction to the minister [that is to Grenville himself]?

A. Soon after my arrival, while the stamping of America was under consideration, and before the bill was brought in.

[172] Q. Would it be most for the interest of Great-Britain, to employ the hands of Virginia in tobacco, or in manufactures?

A. In tobacco to be sure."

Rockingham would not let Grenville's be the final voice Franklin heard. The final exchange became a kind of peroration common in formal oratory.

"[173] Q. What used to be the pride of the Americans?

A. To indulge in the fashions and manufactures of Great-Britain.

[174] Q. What is now their pride?

A. To wear their old cloaths over again, till they can make new ones."

Franklin withdrew.

Buried not far below the surface of Franklin's informative replies was another kind of speech, foreboding, warning, lecturing about the colonial idea of the empire. Franklin could not know what the average colonist thought, not over so vast and so diverse a population. What his miniature essays conveyed instead was an evolving sense of colonial entitlement and a growing fear that British authorities were moving in a different direction. The evolution of these ideas about colonial liberty and British corruption was not linear, nor was it inevitable. Instead, it was irregular, a series of jumps and swerves, as colonial political thinkers responded to what Parliament did, and what the colonials thought parliamentary leaders were thinking. In 1766, this logic of protest thought was still evolving. The full development of it would not appear until a new ministry, led by Frederick, Lord North, took the helm in Westminster.

CHAPTER 5

The Declaratory Act of 1766

Franklin's testimony before Parliament was a media event. Notes of the dialogue were transcribed and published in England and the colonies, and, translated, in France as well. Some in England and the colonies credited Franklin with convincing the Rockingham ministry to repeal the Act, which followed on March 8, 1766 (the king reluctantly signed the bill). In fact, the ministry was looking for a graceful way to retreat before Franklin was invited to aid their deliberations.[64]

To save face and to restate what many opponents and supporters of the Stamp Act agreed on, the Rockingham ministry proposed and Parliament passed the Declaratory Act of March 18, 1766. It was a collective response to the implications of Franklin's testimony. As one member wrote of the debates on the repeal, "A fuller house I don't recollect to have seen, and it is to the honor of Parliament I must add, that I believe there never was a debate so temperate, serious, solemn, and parliamentary, without the least appearance of party or faction . . . intermingling in the argument upon the question on one side or the other." Members agreed that the colonies were not self-governing and could not claim by law what Franklin had asserted existed in fact—a kind of political adulthood quite different from dependency.[65]

"An act for the better securing the dependency of his Majesty's dominions in America upon the crown and parliament of Great Britain.

"Whereas several of the houses of representatives in his Majesty's colonies and plantations in America, have of late, against law, claimed to themselves, or to the general assemblies of the same, the sole and exclusive right of imposing duties and taxes upon his Majesty's subjects in the said colonies and plantations; and have, in pursuance of such claim, passed certain votes, resolutions, and orders, derogatory to the legislative authority of parliament, and inconsistent with the dependency of the said colonies and plantations upon the crown of Great Britain: . . . be it declared . . .

"That the said colonies and plantations in America have been, are, and of right ought to be. subordinate unto, and dependent upon the imperial crown and parliament of Great Britain; and that the King's majesty, by and with the advice and consent of the lords spiritual and temporal, and commons of Great Britain, in parliament assembled, had, has, and of right ought to have, full power and authority to make laws and statutes of sufficient force and validity to bind the colonies and people of America, subjects of the crown of Great Britain, in all cases whatsoever.

"And be it further declared . . . That all resolutions, votes, orders, and proceedings, in any of the said colonies or plantations, whereby the power and authority of the parliament of Great Britain, to make laws and statutes as aforesaid, is denied, or drawn into question, are, and are hereby declared to be, utterly null and void to all intents and purposes whatsoever."

CONCLUSION

Franklin in the Cockpit, 1774

WITH THE REPEAL of the Stamp Act and the passage of the Declaratory Act, colonial protests quieted, but plans for nonimportation of British goods in opposition to the Townshend duties of 1767 on tea and other commodities were almost as disruptive as the protests against the Stamp Act. Grenville continued to insist that he thought the Stamp Act provided for the "honor and safety of the king and his people." Loyal Americans wrote privately to Grenville that they had done their best to support his programs and worried that "The success, since that repeal [of the Stamp Act], which has attended the measures taken in the colonies . . . in opposition to the authority of parliament, may make it more difficult to convince men of their errors than it would have been by enforcing the stamp act."[66]

Franklin remained in Britain, diligently lobbying for high colonial office—perhaps the governorship of Pennsylvania when it should become a royal instead of a proprietary colony. But two visits to the Privy Council chamber, called the cockpit for its architecture's resemblance to the favorite vice of English gamblers (it could also have been called the bear pit for the same reason), ended these hopes. The story behind those visits comprised a dramatic conclusion to Franklin's part in the Stamp Act controversy and turned an imperial jobseeker into a confirmed revolutionary.

In 1768, Governor Francis Bernard and Lieutenant Governor Thomas Hutchinson asked the Privy Council to approve the sending of troops in peacetime to Boston. Bernard was an English lawyer and colonial administrator who had served as New Jersey's royal governor for a year before taking the same job in Massachusetts. He held the latter office from 1759 to 1769, when he was recalled. From then until his death in 1779, he advised the crown on colonial affairs. Hutchinson's family went back to the first settlers of Massachusetts. He was a successful merchant and political moderate when named lieutenant governor in 1759 and chief justice in 1760. A loyalist, he left Boston in 1774 and died in his English exile in 1780. Around both men a faction had grown, including Hutchinson in-law Peter Oliver, who became chief justice in 1769, and Andrew Oliver, the short-term stamp distributor.

Opponents of the faction included James Otis Jr., a lawyer; John and Samuel Adams; and merchant John Hancock.

The Privy Council, composed of the attorney general, solicitor general, and other key legal advisors to the Crown, acceded to Bernard's request, and troops arrived in Boston on October 1, 1768. Irritations and confrontations between the two regiments of regulars and the locals, instigated in part by the Sons of Liberty, exploded in the Boston Massacre of March 5, 1770, during which five men in a street crowd died from gunshot wounds. The trials of the officer of the guard and eight soldiers were major public events in the fall of the year, and though Captain Preston and six of the soldiers were acquitted, and the other two branded on their thumbs for manslaughter, the entire affair inflamed anti-British sentiments.[67]

Hutchinson sent an account of the affair to the Secretary of State for the Southern Department, which, along with the earlier letters to Thomas Whately and other confidants in England (some of which the increasingly worried Hutchinson had composed in cipher), fell into the hands of Franklin in 1773. How they got there remains a mystery, but they had been given to Grenville and were in his possession when he died, in 1770. Franklin read the letters for the first time in early 1773 and later admitted that he was shocked by Hutchinson's views. Determined to prove that the British government was not the cause of the troubles (so he said in his defense), and perhaps unaware of the consternation it would cause, he sent six of the letters back to Boston. There John Adams carried them to the Massachusetts assembly, which condemned them, and on June 15, 1773, they were published in pamphlet form.[68]

The letters that Bernard and Hutchinson sent seemed to Boston Whigs proof positive of a conspiracy against American liberty. Hutchinson's position as royal governor became untenable, and a year later he would be replaced by General Thomas Gage. In the meantime, a mob in Boston had thrown chests of East India Company tea into the harbor in protest against the Tea Act, and Parliament was debating what punitive measures to take against the perpetrators. The Massachusetts legislature petitioned the crown to relent, and when Franklin was summoned to appear in the Cockpit on January 11, 1774, he assumed he was there to explain the petition.

Alexander, Lord Wedderburn, the solicitor general, had other ideas: He held Franklin responsible for the publication of Hutchinson's private correspondence. Learning of the intent of the summons, Franklin sought a delay to find counsel. He did not deny sending the letters back; indeed, he published a defense of his actions. When he reappeared, on January 29, Wedderburn did not give Franklin or his counsel, John Dunning, a chance to present a case or explain themselves. Before a packed house of thirty-five councilors and an audience (including Franklin's younger protégé Edward Bancroft), he accused Franklin of complicity in the publication of the letters and argued that it amounted to a constructive treason (a capital offense in England entailing imperiling the crown). Bancroft later recalled that "The Doctor . . . stood conspicuously erect, without the smallest movement of any part of his body. The muscles of his face had been previously composed as to afford a placid tranquil expression of countenance, and he did not suffer the slightest alteration of it to appear." Wedderburn lectured Franklin for an hour and Franklin left the room, his aspirations for preferment within the empire behind him.[69]

As the following excerpt from Wedderburn's remarks demonstrates, they took the form of a prosecutor giving his summation in a criminal case to the jury. It is full of personal assault on Franklin's motives and character. In one sense, it was what Grenville wanted to say but could not:[70]

"My Lords, you will mark and brand this man, for the honor of this country, Europe, and mankind. He has forfeited all the respect of societies and of men. Into what companies will he hereafter go with an unembarrassed face, or the honest intrepedity of virtue? Men will watch him with a jealous eye; they will hide their papers from him, and lock up their escritoires [desks]. He will henceforth deem it a libel to be called a man of letters . . . But he not only took away the letters from one brother, but kept himself concealed till he nearly occasioned the murder of the other, expressive of the coolest and most deliberate malice, without horror . . . amid these tragical events, of one person nearly killed, of another answerable for the issue, of a worthy governor hurt in his dearest interests; the fate of America is in suspense; here is a man who, with the utmost insensibility of remorse, stands up and avows himself the author of all."

The consensus of Parliament that the colonies were not to determine fiscal policy for themselves, laid alongside Franklin's candid and confident view that the colonists would never henceforth accept rule in which had no part, omened a widening breach between the home country and its North American colonies. Though neither he nor the members of Parliament in 1774 seemed to want it, that breach came. The full and frank dialogue of February 13, 1766 had shown how far apart the two sides were a full decade before Virginia's Richard Henry Lee rode into Philadelphia and presented the Continental Congress with Virginia's proposal for American independence.

Ironically, a few weeks before Lee returned to Philadelphia, Scottish economist Adam Smith proposed a moderate solution to the crisis. Watching from his place as professor of moral economy at the University of Edinburgh, well aware of the controversy over stamped paper ten years earlier and Franklin's report to Parliament, Smith argued that the individual should surrender his self-interest to the general interest or the public interest when it promoted long-term benefits for all. The "general interest of the country" would promote the particular interests of buyers and sellers, producers and consumers. At the same time, he knew that the colonists would never trust this formula unless they had seats in Parliament. If "the people on the other side of the water are afraid, lest their distance from the seat of government might expose them to many oppressions. . . . their representatives in

Parliament, of which the number from the first ought to be considerable, would easily be able to protect them from all oppression." But Smith's words were published on March 9, 1776, and by then both sides were too bent on their diverging courses to listen to him.[71]

Looking back at Franklin's interview, one can and perhaps should ask if he meant what he said, or was slyly deflecting criticism of the colonies by telling America's friends in Parliament what they wanted—or at least needed—to hear? Asking whether Franklin meant what he said is not quite the same as taking him at his word. This apparent puzzle needs some explanation, because unraveling it is an essential part of scholarly reading of primary sources. Even if one were confident that one understood what Franklin was trying to convey, that confidence does not automatically extend to understanding what Franklin was trying to do. He was a performer, a master of words. No doubt he had some idea in advance of both the hostile and the friendly questions. His answers had a scripted quality, as though he had practiced many of them in advance. One suspects he did. To persuade doubters, reassure supporters, and counter opponents he must choose the right words. Frankness was less important than the appearance of frankness in such a performance. With this in mind, the scholar and the student must see and hear the examination as well as read it. That is the lesson for deciphering all primary sources—make the words come alive by making the setting, the actors, and issues come alive.

Bibliographical Essay

IN 1959, SIX years after he and his wife Helen Morgan wrote the first edition of *The Stamp Act Crisis: Prologue to Revolution* (Chapel Hill: University of North Carolina Press, 1953), Edmund Morgan collected some of the documentary evidence and published it in W.W. Norton's "Documentary Problems in Early American History" series for the Institute of Early American History and Culture (now the Omohundro Institute) at Williamsburg. The series did not last long (it ended in 1974, with only five volumes), but Morgan's *Prologue to Revolution: Sources and Documents on the Stamp Act Crisis, 1764–1766* (New York: Norton, 1959), would become the model for the much more successful J. B. Wiley and Sons, and later Houghton Mifflin, "Problems in American History" series.

Morgan was characteristically modest in his assessment of the classroom use of the collection: "Even the briefer collections of source problems are no substitute for a continuous narrative and if used without a text are likely to leave the student with no sense of chronology. But if he can plunge into a close study at one or two points, he may emerge with an understanding of historical problems and historical method that no amount of secondary works can give him." With this in mind, one could say that the "Dialogues in History" series itself is something like the grandchild of the "Documentary Problems" series.

The Franklin examination was reexamined by Lawrence H. Gipson in "The Great Debate in the Committee of the Whole House of Commons on the Stamp Act, 1766, as reported by Nathaniel Ryder," *Pennsylvania Magazine of History and Biography* 86 (1962), 10–41. Gipson was a historian of the Seven Years' War whose encyclopedic nine-volume *British Empire before the American Revolution* (1936–1970) was the gold standard. A more recent and similarly superb account of Franklin in Parliament appears in the Leonard W. Labaree et al., eds., *Papers of Benjamin Franklin* (New Haven: Yale University Press, 1969), 13: 124–129. The edition of the examination, merging manuscript with print versions, follows on pages 129–145.

On the Stamp Act, the first of the modern accounts is Edmund S. and Helen M. Morgan, *The Stamp Act Crisis: Prologue to Revolution* (Chapel Hill: University of North Carolina Press, 1953), reprinted with a new preface in 1995. Morgan believed that the protests were really about what the Americans said they were about: Taxation without consent violated the English constitution and, because the protestors saw their rights coming from that source, the Stamp Act violated the rights of the colonists. Written at the height of the Cold War, one can read the book as a reaffirmation of Americans' deep commitment to basic rights like the right to property. The ironic fact of a Patrick Henry passionately defending liberty when he not only owned but traded slaves was not a part of the Morgans' analysis.

From 1765 to 1770, there were over a hundred pamphlets and broadsides on the Act, some of whose authors concealed their identities (to prevent prosecution for seditious libel) behind pen names like Junius Americanus. The first of these, by Connecticut's Thomas Fitch, explaining why Britain should not impose direct taxes on the colonies, was among the most temperate. Some of these were collected in the Old North Pamphlet series, edited first by Samuel Eliot Morrison and later by Bernard Bailyn, both professors at Harvard. The pamphlets became the basis for Bailyn's prize-winning *Ideological Origins of the American Revolution* (Cambridge, MA: Harvard University Press, 1967). Bailyn too took the protestors at their word, but unlike Morgan, saw the foundational ideas of the protest in the publications of a radical fringe group in England and its American correspondents.

There is no other full-dress scholarly account of the Stamp Act protests, but it is explored in larger works on the revolutionary crisis. The interpretations range from Howard Zinn's assertion that the root of the protest was class anger, with lower-class mobs manipulated by colonial elites to deflect animosity from them to the British administration (*A People's History of the United States* [New York: Harper, 2009], 61), to Gordon Wood's belief that the protests were led by patriots who believed that liberty and hierarchy were compatible (*The Radicalism of the American Revolution* [New York: Knopf, 1992], 61–62). For Wood, the animus was not class anger but personal pique. Pauline Maier took the middle ground when she argued that the protests were only a start in the process of resistance, with all the patriots "looking for guidance" (*From Resistance to Revolution: Colonial Radicals and the Development of American Opposition to Britain, 1765–1776* [New York: Norton, 1992], 53). Wood and Maier were students of Bernard Bailyn.

The larger context of American protests is one of the most voluminous and still controverted issues in American historical writing. Some historians see the coming of the Revolution as a top-down affair, while others see it rising from the bottom up. The gap between these schools grows wider with each of their publications. As uncompromising toward one another's views as the Whigs and Tories were before the final breach with Britain, leading scholars' accounts leave the reader wondering what really happened. If only one could see it for oneself! A sampling: a Revolution from the top down: Bailyn, *Ideological Origins of the American Revolution*; Jack

Rakove, *Revolutionaries: A New History of the Invention of America* (New York: Houghton Mifflin, 2010); and Wood's *Radicalism of the American Revolution*; from the bottom up, T. H. Breen, *American Insurgents, American Patriots: The Revolution of the American People* (New York: Hill and Wang, 2010); Edward Countryman, *The American Revolution: Revised Edition* (New York: Hill and Wang, 2003); and Gary Nash, *The Unknown American Revolution: The Unruly Birth of Democracy and the Struggle to Create America* (New York: Viking, 2005).

Whatever the larger theoretical orientation of the accounts, the Stamp Act protests play a central role in them. For example, Robert Middlekauff, *The Glorious Cause: The American Revolution, 1763–1789* (New York: Oxford University Press, 2007), 130, regarded the protests as important because they gave impetus to the theory that a conspiracy existed in the Grenville ministry against American liberties. Narrative histories tend to give the Act and the protests even more of a role in the coming of the Revolution. Benson Bobrick, *Angel in the Whirlwind: The Triumph of the American Revolution* (New York: Penguin, 1997), 71, termed the Stamp Act "notorious", a key event in the sequence of protests. John Ferling, *A Leap in the Dark: The Struggle to Create the American Republic* (New York: Oxford University Press, 2003), 40, argued that the Stamp Act protests gave a stamp of approval to direct crowd action, bringing the common people into the streets as political players.

The two central players in the examination of Franklin shared an Anglo-American, trans-Atlantic stage, but later historians have not emphasized this commonality, much less produced anything like a dual biography of the two men. Instead, Franklin has been seen as the essential American, though he spent a good deal of his life in England, and Grenville as an English politician, although his fate and that of the empire were indissolubly tied. On Franklin as a transatlantic figure, see Peter Charles Hoffer, *When Benjamin Franklin Met the Reverend Whitefield* (Baltimore: Johns Hopkins University Press, 2012).

Franklin is not without his critics, but far more common are admiring biographers. Carl Van Doren's *Benjamin Franklin* (New York: Viking, 1938), a Pulitzer Prize-winning giant (over 830 pages), included a good selection of Franklin's own writing. Van Doren, a professor of American literature at Columbia University, viewed Franklin as one of the founding fathers of American letters as well as the new republic. He lionized his subject: "In any age, Franklin would have been great" (782). H. W. Brands' *The First American: The Life and Times of Benjamin Franklin* (New York: Doubleday, 2000) is immensely detailed and balanced. Edwin S. Gaustad's compact *Benjamin Franklin* (New York: Oxford University Press, 2006) has the virtues of succinctness and a fine eye for the telling short quotation. Walter Isaacson's *Benjamin Franklin: A Life* (New York: Simon and Schuster, 2004) is a big, breezy, highly anecdotal account of the man by a highly successful journalist who saw much of himself in Franklin. The three volumes of J. A. Leo Lemay's *The Life of Benjamin Franklin* (Philadelphia: University of Pennsylvania Press, 2006) are compendious, highly complimentary to its subject, though a somewhat disorderly account of Franklin from his birth to 1757. Edmund S. Morgan's *Benjamin Franklin* (New Haven: Yale University Press, 2003) is a relatively short (350 pages) musing on Franklin and his times. Morgan, like Lemay, edited a volume of Franklin's writings. Gordon S. Wood has a distinctive take on Franklin in *The Americanization of Benjamin Franklin* (New York: Penguin, 2004). In a sense, he is out to debunk the heroic mythology and finds instead a striver seeking to become a gentleman (which he does), who then tries to become an imperial power broker (in which quest he embarrassingly fails), and almost by default becomes a patriot and founding father. Esmond Wright's *Franklin of Philadelphia* (Cambridge, MA: Harvard University Press, 1986) is a cool but not distant assessment of Franklin by a leading English historian. It finds the many paradoxes in the subject's life and concludes that Franklin remains elusive because he wanted it that way. More recent works, like David Waldstreicher, *Runaway America: Benjamin Franklin, Slavery, and the American Revolution* (New York: Hill and Wang, 2004), and Gary B. Nash, *the Unknown American Revolution: The Unruly Birth of Democracy and the Struggle to Create America* (New York: Viking, 2005), offer a far more damaging view of Franklin.

All of these biographies are largely based on same set of sources. Jared Sparks was the first editor of Franklin's letters and essays, in 1836. Sparks, a minister by training and a moralist by inclination, was a documentary editor and biographer as well. He had no hesitation about leaving out parts of letters he considered injurious to the reputation of the authors or changing a word here and there for the same purpose. The authoritative modern edition of the Franklin papers is the Yale University-American Philosophical Society *Papers of Benjamin Franklin*, 36 volumes (New Haven: Yale University Press, 1959–1999). It was first edited by Leonard Labaree and then volumes 15 to 26 were edited by W. B. Willcox; volume 27 was edited by Claude A. Lopez; volumes 28 to 35 were edited by Barbara B. Oberg; and volume 36 was edited by Ellen R. Cohn. These are models of their kind, with headnotes and citations that explain terms, fill in details, and otherwise illuminate an illuminating life. The entire thirty-six-volume edition (less the editors' extensive and very valuable annotation) is online in very usable format at www.franklinpapers.org/franklin/framedVolumes.jsp.

Two more recent essays touch on Franklin in England. They are Hoffer, *When Benjamin Franklin Met the Reverend Whitefield* and Sheila L. Skemp, *The Making of a Patriot: Benjamin Franklin in the Cockpit* (New York: Oxford University Press, 2012).

There is very small cottage industry on Grenville: a revised dissertation, Allan S. Johnson, *A Prologue to Revolution: The Political Career of George Grenville, 1712–1770* (Lanham, MD: University Press of America, 1997); Philip Lawson, *George Grenville: A Political Life* (Oxford, UK: Oxford University Press, 1984); and another revised dissertation, John L. Bullion, *A Great and Necessary Measure, George Grenville and the Genesis of the Stamp Act, 1763–1765* (Columbia, MO: University of Missouri Press, 1982). A four-volume edition of Grenville's letters appeared as *The Grenville Papers*, ed. William James Smith (London: Murray, 1853).

Grenville appears in other works on eighteenth-century British history and politics, of course, for example Ian R. Christie, *Myth and Reality in Late Eighteenth-Century English Politics* (Berkeley: University of California Press, 1970); Robert Harris, *Politics and the Nation: Britain in the Mid-Eighteenth Century* (Oxford, UK: Oxford University Press, 2002); and J. Steven Watson, *The Reign of George III, 1760–1815* (Oxford, UK: Oxford University Press, 1960).

The masterwork on Thomas Hutchinson, whose shadow falls over all of this story, is Bernard Bailyn, *The Ordeal of Thomas Hutchinson* (Cambridge, MA: Harvard University Press, 1974).

Endnotes

1. Gordon S. Wood, *The Americanization of Benjamin Franklin* (New York: Penguin, 2004), 119–120.

2. Fred Anderson, *Crucible of War: The Seven Years War and the Fate of Empire in British America, 1754–1766* (New York: Knopf, 2000), 557–571; Tony Hayter, "The Army and the First British Empire" in David Chandler, ed., *The Oxford History of the British Army* (New York: Oxford University Press, 1996), 124.

3. Eliga Gould, *The Persistence of Empire: British Political Culture in the Age of the American Revolution* (Chapel Hill: University of North Carolina Press, 2000), 110–122.

4. Edmund S. Morgan and Helen M. Morgan, *The Stamp Act Crisis: Prologue to Revolution,* rev. ed. (Chapel Hill: University of North Carolina Press, 1995), 28; J. Steven Watson, *The Reign of George III, 1760–1815* (Oxford, UK: Oxford University Press, 1960), 90–92, 96–98.

5. Edmund Morgan, "The Postponement of the Stamp Act." *William and Mary Quarterly* 3rd ser. 7 (July 1950), 352–393, quotation on p. 358.

6. Morgan and Morgan, *Prologue to Revolution: Sources and Documents on the Stamp Act Crisis, 1764–1766* (New York: Norton, 1959), 35–43.

7. Wood, *Americanization*, 108.

8. The best single volume on the Stamp Act controversy is still Edmund S. and Helen M. Morgan, *The Stamp Act Crisis: Prologue to Revolution,* rev. ed. (Chapel Hill: University of North Carolina Press, 1995).

9. Pauline Maier, in *From Resistance to Revolution: Colonial Radicals and the Development of American Opposition to Britain, 1765–1776* (New York: Knopf, 1972), 77–100, argues that the actual organization arose out of the demonstrations rather than the planning of them.

10. *Newport Mercury*, August 26, 1765, quoted in Robert Blair St. George, *Conversing by Signs: Poetics of Implication in Colonial New England* (Chapel Hill: University of North Carolina Press, 1998), 259.

11. David W. Conroy, *In Public Houses: Drink and the Revolution of Authority in Colonial Massachusetts* (Chapel Hill: University of North Carolina Press, 1995), 257–258, 262–263; Dirk Hoerder, *Crowd Action in Revolutionary Massachusetts* (New York: Academic Press, 1977), 108.

12. Bernard to Halifax, August 15, 1765, in Morgan, ed., *Prologue*, 107–108.

13. Thomas Hutchinson to Richard Jackson, August 30, 1765, in Morgan, ed., *Prologue*, 108–109.

14. H.W. Brands, *First American: The Life and Times of Benjamin Franklin* (New York: Doubleday, 2000), 367, quotation on p. 368.

15. P. J. Kulishek, "Charles Watson-Wentworth," in Gerald Newman and Leslie Ellen Brown, eds., *Britain in the Hanoverian Age, 1714–1837: An Encyclopedia* (London: Taylor and Francis, 1997), 605–606.

16. See, e.g., the uses of language cited in Gary B. Nash, *The Unknown American Revolution: The Unruly Birth of Democracy and the Struggle to Create America* (New York: Penguin, 2005), 78, Sandra M. Gustafson, *Eloquence is Power: Oratory and Performance in Early America* (Chapel Hill: University of North Carolina Press, 2000), 145, and Gordon S. Wood, *The Radicalism of the American Revolution* (New York: Knopf, 1990), 91.

17. Bernard Bailyn, *The Ideological Origins of the American Revolution* (Cambridge, MA: Harvard University Press, 1967), xiii; Philip Davidson, *Propaganda and the American Revolution* (Chapel Hill: University of North Carolina Press, 1941), 3 and after; Quentin Skinner, *Visions of Politics: Regarding Method* (Cambridge, UK: Cambridge University Press, 2002), 1:4–5 and after.

18. *Proceedings and Debates of the British Parliaments Respecting North America, 1754–1783*, eds. R. C. Simmons & P. D. G. Thomas (Millwood, NY: Kraus International Publications, 1983), 2: 8–17; Joanna Innes, "Legislation and Public Participation, 1760–1830" in David Lemmings, ed., *The British and Their Laws in the Eighteenth Century* (London: Boydell, 2005), 108–109.

19. Thomas C. Barrow, "Background to the Grenville Program, 1757–1763." *William and Mary Quarterly* 3rd ser. 22 (1965), 93–104; Whately quoted in Ian R. Christie, "A Vision of Empire: Thomas Whately and the Regulations Lately Made Concerning the Colonies" *English Historical Review* 113 (1998), 304.

20. On the notion of salutary neglect, see James Henretta, *Salutary Neglect: Colonial Administration Under the Duke of Newcastle* (Princeton: Princeton University Press, 1972).

21. Duties in American Colonies Act, March 22, 1765; 5 George III, c. 12; D. E. Schremmer, "Taxation and Public Finance: Britain, France, and Germany" in Peter Mathias and Sidney Pollard, eds., *The Cambridge Economic History of Europe: The Industrial Economies: The Development of Economic and Social Policies* (Cambridge, UK: Cambridge University Press, 1989), 8:317.

22. Richard R. Beeman, *The Varieties of Political Experience in Eighteenth-Century America* (Philadelphia: University of Pennsylvania Press, 2004), 48–49.

23. John P. Kennedy, ed., *Journals of the House of Burgesses of Virginia, 1761–1765* (Richmond: Waddey, 1907), 360.

24. Kennedy, ed., *Journals*, lxvii. On the various sources of Henry's purported comment, see Moses Coit Tyler, *Patrick Henry* (Boston: Houghton Mifflin, 1898), 73 n. 1.

25. J. R. Bartlett, ed., *Records of the Colony of Rhode Island* (Providence: A.C. Greene, for the Legislature of the State of Rhode Island 1856–1863), 6: 452. On the spread of Henry's resolutions, see Morgan and Morgan, *Stamp Act Crisis*, 132.

26. Americanus, "Letter to the Editor," *New York Gazette*, August 15, 1765. On Galloway, Wallace Brown, *The Good Americans: The Loyalists in the American Revolution* (New York: Morrow, 1969), 32–33 and after.

27. *Proceedings of the Congress at New York* (Annapolis, 1766), 15–16.

28. John Dickinson, *Friends and Countrymen, The Critical Time is Now Come* (Philadelphia, 1765).

29. Entry for December 18, 1765, *Diary and Autobiography of John Adams*, ed. Lyman H. Butterfield (Cambridge, MA: Harvard University Press, 1961), 1:265.

30. "Pacificus," *London Gazetteer and Daily Advertiser*, November 13, 1765. Jack P. Greene opined that the protests in the colonies got "a mixed reception" in England. *Peripheries and Center: Constitutional Development in the Extended Polities of the British Empire and the United States* (Athens: University of Georgia Press, 1986), 97.

31. William Cobbett, ed., *The Parliamentary History of England* (London: Hansard, 1813), 16: 97–108.

32. Ralph Frasca, "Benjamin Franklin's Printing Network and the Stamp Act." *Pennsylvania History* 71 (2004), 403–419.

33. See, e.g., Walter L. Dorn, *The Rise of Modern Europe: Competition for Empire, 1740–1763* (New York: Harper, 1940), 221–236.

34. Wood, *Americanization*, 113.

35. Brands, *The First American*, 368.

36. On Franklin the public relations agent for Franklin, see David Waldstreicher, *Runaway America: Benjamin Franklin, Slavery, and the American Revolution* (New York: Hill and Wang, 2004), 184.

37. George Whitefield quoted in Harry S. Stout, *The Divine Dramatist: George Whitefield and the Rise of Modern Evangelism* (Grand Rapids, MI: Eerdmans, 1991), 263.

38. Frasca, "Benjamin Franklin's Printing Network and the Stamp Act," 406, 407, 409, 410; Franklin to the *Gazetteer and New Daily Advertiser*, December 28, 1765.

39. Tal Golan, *Laws of Men and Laws of Nature: The History of Scientific Expert Testimony in England and America* (Cambridge, MA: Harvard University Press, 2004), 16.

40. Kirstin Olsen, *Daily Life in Eighteenth-Century England* (Santa Barbara, CA: Greenwood, 1999), 6–7.

41. Hannah Barker, *Newspapers, Politics, and Public Opinion in Late Eighteenth-Century England* (Oxford, UK: Oxford University Press, 1982), 17, 19; Jeremy Black, *The English Press in the Eighteenth Century* (London: Taylor and Francis, 1987), 129.

42. See, e.g., Beeman, *The Varieties of Political Experience in Eighteenth-Century America*, 52 and after.

43. Headnote, "Examination before the Committee of the Whole of the House of Commons," in Leonard W. Labaree et al., eds., *The Papers of Benjamin Franklin* (New Haven: Yale University Press, 1969-) 13:124–129.

44. Benjamin Franklin, "Examination before the Committee of the Whole of the House of Commons" February 13, 1766, in Labaree et al., eds., *The Papers of Benjamin Franklin*, 13: 129–145.

45. Beeman, *The Varieties of Political Experience in Eighteenth-Century America*, passim.

46. Peter Silver, *Our Savage Neighbors: How Indian War Transformed Early America* (New York: Norton, 2007), 35–36; Franklin, *Plain Truth: Serious Considerations on the Present State of the City of Philadelphia and the Province of Pennsylvania* (Philadelphia: B. Franklin, 1747), 3–10.

47. On Pitt, Conway, and the Stamp Act repeal debates, see Fred Anderson, *Crucible of War: The Seven Years War and the Fate of British Empire in America, 1754–1766* (New York: Knopf, 2000), 698–701.

48. Patricia Cline Cohen, *A Calculating People: The Spread of Numeracy in Early America* (Chicago: University of Chicago Press, 1983), 84–85.

49. For Franklin's "Hints" that a tax would be acceptable, see Timothy J. Shannon, *Indians and Colonists at the Crossroads of Empire: The Albany Congress of 1754* (Ithaca, NY: Cornell University Press, 2002), 179–180.

50. See, in general, Oliver Morton Dickerson, *The Navigation Acts and the American Revolution* (Philadelphia: University of Pennsylvania Press, 1974).

51. Looking ahead: Sheila L. Skemp, *The Making of a Patriot: Benjamin Franklin at the Cockpit* (New York: Oxford University Press, 2012), 88.

52. On Franklin's ambitions, Wood, *Americanization*, 95.

53. In a very controversial book, historian Michael Bellesiles argued that few colonial households had working firearms. See *Arming America: The Making of a National Gun Culture* (New York: Knopf, 2000). Much of the data in that book was either fabricated or irreproducible. Bellesiles himself replaced the tables in that book with new tables from different primary sources in his 2003 version with Soft Skull Press. His evasions and the investigation into them are summarized in Peter Charles Hoffer, *Past Imperfect*, rev. ed. (New York: Public Affairs Press, 2007), 141–171.

54. T. H. Breen, *The Marketplace of Revolution: How Consumer Politics Shaped American Independence* (New York: Oxford University Press, 2004), 298–299.

55. Andrew Jackson O'Shaughnessy, *An Empire Divided: The American Revolution and the British Caribbean* (Philadelphia: University of Pennsylvania Press, 2000), 72.

56. John Gilbert McCurdy, *Citizen Bachelors: Manhood and the Creation of the United States* (Ithaca, NY: Cornell University Press, 2009), 61–62.

57. On the connection between colonial and English merchants, see, e.g., Arthur M. Schlesinger, *The Colonial Merchants and the American Revolution* (New York: Columbia University Press, 1918), 50–90 and Cathy Matson, *Merchants and Empire: Trading in Colonial New York* (Baltimore: Johns Hopkins University Press, 2002), 215–312.

58. The story goes like this: Archbishop of Canterbury John Morton was collecting taxes in fifteenth-century England. He opined that a man who seemed to be living within his means must be saving, so he could pay taxes from his savings. A man who lived in luxury must be rich, and so he too could pay taxes.

59. John Philip Reid, *In Defiance of the Law: The Standing-Army Controversy, the Two Constitutions, and the Coming of the American Revolution* (Chapel Hill: University of North Carolina Press, 1981), 4, 45.

60. Edmund Burke was a supporter of colonial rights and would remain so throughout the protests. See, e.g., Peter James Stanlis, *Edmund Burke: The Enlightenment and Revolution* (New York: Transaction, 1991), 19–22.

61. Bernard Bailyn, *The Ordeal of Thomas Hutchinson* (Cambridge, MA: Harvard University Press, 1974), 88–89; Shannon, 13, 102.

62. The Stamp Act brought these theories to a head, see, e.g., Bernard Bailyn, *Faces of Revolution: Personalities and Themes in the Struggle for American Independence* (New York: Knopf, 1990), 125–136. But Franklin was not a deep theorist: He preferred useful information to abstract theorizing. He did understand, however, that a cultural transformation was under way among colonial reading public, and that the word "American" as in "British American" was gaining traction as a proud depiction of what today would be called American exceptionalism.

63. See, generally, John Phillip Reid, *The Constitutional History of the American Revolution: The Authority to Tax* (Madison: University of Wisconsin Press, 1987).

64. Wood, *Americanization*, 120–121; Brands, *First American*, 374.

65. Charles Garth to ____ March 5, 1766, printed in *Maryland Historical Magazine* 6 (1911), 305; The Declaratory Act of March 18, 1766, 6 Geo. III c.12; Statutes at Large, 27: 19–20.

66. George Grenville to Thomas Whately, July 30, 1767; Cadwallader Colden to George Grenville, October 22, 1768, in William James Smith, ed., *The Grenville Papers* (London: Murray, 1853), 4: 125–126; 388.

67. Hiller B. Zobel, *The Boston Massacre* (New York: Norton, 1970), 268, 281, 293.

68. Bailyn, *Hutchinson*, 222–242.

69. Account from Skemp, *The Making of a Patriot*; 2–8; quotation from the eyewitness account of Edward Bancroft, in Thomas J. Schaeper, *Edward Bancroft: Scientist, Author, Spy* (New Haven: Yale University Press, 2011), 40.

70. Massachusetts Historical Society, *Historical Collections* 2: 147–148.

71. Adam Smith, *Inquiry into the Wealth of Nations* [1776] (New York: Collier, 1902), part II: 394.

Credits

PHOTO CREDITS

Introduction

Page 2: © National Portrait Gallery, London; page 5: Courtesy of the Library of Congress, LC-USZ61-449; page 7: Thomas Hutchinson (1711–80) 1741 (oil on canvas), Truman, Edward (18th century)/© Massachusetts Historical Society, Boston, MA, USA/Bridgeman Images; page 9: Portrait of Benjamin Franklin by Michael J. Deas © 2003.

Chapter 4

Page 31: House of Commons Interior before the fire of 1834, from Ackermann's 'Microcosm of London', Rowlandson, T. (1756–1827) & Pugin, A.C. (1762–1832)/British Library, London, UK/© British Library Board. All Rights Reserved/Bridgeman Images.

Index